WHOLENESS
X
PRIORITY

SET IN SOUL

THIS JOURNAL BELONGS TO

_____

DEDICATED TO YOUR TODAY.
THE DAY YOU DECIDED
TO THROW AWAY YOUR EXCUSES
AND START SOMETHING NEW.

TABLE OF
CONTENTS

HOW TO USE THIS JOURNAL

Wholeness x Priority is a health journal that focuses on the health of the mind, body and spirit. There is an understanding that your health is not only based on what you put into your body, but also on the habits you have formed, your thoughts, and how you treat yourself. With this journal, you will be able to keep track of your mental, physical, and emotional health. By taking the time to keep track of your overall health, you will be able to see what parts of you need more attention before it begins to affect other aspects of your life. When you make every aspect of your health a priority, you will begin to see things blossoming within and outside of you. In this manner, you will be comfortable in your own skin and function at your best.

Because you understand the importance of taking care of every facet of your health, it is recommended that you use this journal daily. Fill out the morning sections early each day, and complete the remaining prompts at night. Take a look at what you wrote, and reflect on the actions that you were most proud of as well as the things you can improve on. By paying attention to your needs and filling out this journal, you will notice your self-confidence and self-awareness improve. You will feel and look rejuvenated. You will glow from the inside out. Let this journal be an avenue to your truth. Live in your greatness. You have a mission, and that mission is to make wholeness a priority. The time to start is now.

MY GO-TOS AND VISITS

(Write The Name, Address, And Phone Numbers As Well
As Your Last Visit And Next)

My Physician: _____

_____

_____

My Dentist: _____

_____

_____

My Optometrist Or Ophthalmologist: _____

_____

_____

My Dermatologist: _____

_____

_____

MY GO-TOS AND VISITS

My Gynecologist: _____

_____

_____

My Urologist: _____

_____

_____

My Nutritionist: _____

_____

_____

Other Doctors That I See: _____

_____

_____

My Spiritual Adviser:_____

_____

_____

MY GO-TOS AND VISITS

My Personal Trainer: _____

_____

_____

The Gym That I Am A Member Of: _____

_____

_____

Social Influencers And Others Who Inspire Me To Cook: _____

_____

_____

Social Influencers And Others Who Inspire Me To Eat Healthier Meals: __

_____

_____

Social Influencers And Others Who Inspire Me To Workout: _____

_____

_____

THE KEY TO MY PHYSICAL WELLBEING

THE KEY TO MY PHYSICAL WELLBEING

My Current Age:

My Height:

My Current Weight:

My Body Type:

My Blood Type:

THE KEY TO MY PHYSICAL WELLBEING

My Cholesterol Level:

Current Medications That I Take:

My Bowel Movements Are:

My Blood Pressure Level:

Annual Screenings That I Need:

THE KEY TO MY PHYSICAL WELLBEING

Chronic Illnesses That I Suffer From:

Sexually Transmitted Diseases I Currently Have Or Have Had (State Them If Applicable And How You Are Treating Them):

I Experience Headaches And Migraines (State How Often If Applicable To You):

I Am Allergic To:

My Body Feels:

THE KEY TO MY PHYSICAL WELLBEING

I Am Physically Able To:

I Am Physically Unable To:

I Was Once Able To:

Injuries I Suffer From:

Skin Conditions I Have:

THE KEY TO MY PHYSICAL WELLBEING

I Currently Feel Pain (Name The Pain And It's Location):

The Pain Mentioned Above Started:

The Pain Mentioned Above Is Due To:

What I Would Like To Change:

I Know That I Can:

THE KEY TO MY PHYSICAL WELLBEING

I Would Like To Be Able To:

What I Currently Love About My Body:

How Much Weight Do I Want To Gain/Lose?

I Gained/Lost Weight Due To:

My Physical Health Affects My:

THE KEY TO MY PHYSICAL WELLBEING

What Would Truly Make Me Happy?

Once I Reach My First Goal, I Will:

I Like To Eat Until I Am:

My Typical Breakfast Consist Of:

My Typical Lunch Consists Of:

THE KEY TO MY PHYSICAL WELLBEING

My Typical Dinner Consists Of:

Typical Foods I Like To Snack On Are:

My Favorite Meal Is:

My Favorite Vegetable Is:

My Favorite Fruit Is:

THE KEY TO MY PHYSICAL WELLBEING

The Last Time I Was Sick (State The Details...i.e When, Symptoms, Illness, How You Felt And So On):

I Often Get Sick (State How Many Times And/Or When):

I Want To Eat Healthy Because:

Currently My Diet Consists Of:

I Can Be Healthier By:

THE KEY TO MY PHYSICAL WELLBEING

The Excuses I Will Stop Repeating That Keep Me From Being My Best Self Are:

I Currently Love To Cook:

I Currently Eat Out (State How Many Times And Where):

After Eating A Healthy Meal, I Feel:

After Eating An Unhealthy Meal, I Feel:

THE KEY TO MY PHYSICAL WELLBEING

The Vitamins I Currently Take Are:

I Would Currently Describe My Water Intake To Be:

I Am Interested In Being:

My Family Has A History Of:

When It Comes To My Scars, I Feel:

THE KEY TO MY PHYSICAL WELLBEING

When It Comes To My Freckles, I Feel:

When It Comes To My Beauty Marks, I Feel:

My Current Activities That Keep Me Active Are:

I Currently Work Out (State How Often And Where):

Everyday I Wake Up Feeling Physically:

THE KEY TO MY PHYSICAL WELLBEING

I Am Physically:

When I Look At Myself In The Mirror, I Believe I Am:

When I Look At Myself In The Mirror, I Like Seeing:

Five Words I Would Use To Describe My Physical Appearance:

My Current Hygiene Routine:

THE KEY TO MY PHYSICAL WELLBEING

My Past Medical Conditions:

I Have Always Physically Felt:

Vaccinations I Have Received:

The Kinds Of Blood Work That I Had Done Within The Last Two Years And Their Results:

THE KEY TO MY MENTAL WELLBEING

THE KEY TO MY MENTAL WELLBEING

I Have Always Known:

I Have Always Believed:

I Have Evolved Mentally By:

I Currently Stimulate My Mind With:

My Past Has Taught Me:

THE KEY TO MY MENTAL WELLBEING

My Present Is Teaching Me:

My Daily Constant Thoughts Are:

I Fear:

I Know I Can:

All My Life, I Have Heard:

THE KEY TO MY MENTAL WELLBEING

I Pay Attention To:

Someone Important To Me Taught Me:

I Currently Started Believing:

I Focus On:

It Hurts Me When I Think About:

THE KEY TO MY MENTAL WELLBEING

I Wish I Can:

It's Hard For Me:

It's Hard For Me To Accept:

I Have Overcome:

I Will Overcome:

THE KEY TO MY MENTAL WELLBEING

My Thoughts Cause Me To:

What Has Been Stressing Me:

The Steps I Will Take To Eliminate My Stress:

Is it Worth It (The Steps You Will Take)?

The Beliefs That I Have Held On To That Have Hurt Me:

THE KEY TO MY MENTAL WELLBEING

What I Worry About The Most:

What Makes Me Happy?

What Makes Me Cry?

What Frustrates Me?

I Am Anixous About:

THE KEY TO MY MENTAL WELLBEING

What I Currently Envision For Myself:

What I Want To Envision For Myself:

I Am Really Good At:

I Have Realized:

I Remember Feeling:

THE KEY TO MY MENTAL WELLBEING

When I Am In Pain I:

My Breaking Point Is:

I Know I Am:

The Negative Thoughts I Hold On To:

I Know That Once I Let Go Of These Negative Thoughts I:

THE KEY TO MY MENTAL WELLBEING

I Am Currently Focused On:

I Know I Will:

Healthy Changes I Have Made In My Life:

Unhealthy Changes I Have Made In My Life:

Healthy Habits I Have Formed In The Past Year:

THE KEY TO MY MENTAL WELLBEING

Unhealthy Habits I Have Formed In The Past Year:

Things I Do To Support My Emotional Wellbeing:

When I Am Sad, I Cheer Myself Up By:

When I Am Angry Or Anxious, I Calm Myself Down By:

I Cry The Hardest When I Think About:

THE KEY TO MY MENTAL WELLBEING

I Laugh The Hardest When I Think About:

I Feel Joy When I Think About:

This Past Year I Have Taken Care Of Myself By Doing:

I Have Always Felt:

Mental Illnesses That Run In My Family:

THE WEALTH IN
MY HEALTH

THE WEALTH IN MY HEALTH

Today: Mood:

Today's Physical Goal: Today I Need:

Today I Am Showing Appreciation To My   I Will Give Myself What I Need Today By:
Body By:

Today I Am Choosing To Believe: I Know I Do Not Need:

Today I Am Replacing An Old Belief With   Today's Physical Activity Is:
This New Belief (State The New Belief):

I Will Support My New Beliefs By: Today I Am Opening Up My Heart And
                                                Mind To:

Today's Blood Pressure: _____ Today's Sugar Count: _____

38   Continue To The Next Page

THE WEALTH IN MY HEALTH
NIGHT ACTIONS AND THOUGHTS

For Breakfast Today I Had:

For Lunch Today I Had:

For Dinner Today I Had:

Today I Snacked On:

Today's Water Intake:

Today's Supplements Were:

Today's Exercise/Physical Activity Was
(State What It Was And For How Long):

Today's Compliment To Myself:

Today I Imagined Myself:

Although I Wanted To

_____, I

_____

_____.

A Characteristic That I Am Choosing To
Improve On:

Affirmation #1: I Am Getting Healthier And Healthier. I Am
Feeling Better And Better.

39

THE WEALTH IN MY HEALTH

Today: Mood:

Today's Physical Goal: Today I Need:

Today I Am Showing Appreciation To My   I Will Give Myself What I Need Today By:
Body By:

Today I Am Choosing To Believe: I Know I Do Not Need:

Today I Am Replacing An Old Belief With   Today's Physical Activity Is:
This New Belief (State The New Belief):

I Will Support My New Beliefs By: Today I Am Opening Up My Heart And
                                                    Mind To:

Today's Blood Pressure: _____ Today's Sugar Count: _____

40   Continue To The Next Page

THE WEALTH IN MY HEALTH

For Breakfast Today I Had:

Today's Exercise/Physical Activity Was (State What It Was And For How Long):

For Lunch Today I Had:

Today's Compliment To Myself:

For Dinner Today I Had:

Today I Imagined Myself:

Today I Snacked On:

Although I Wanted To

_____, I

Today's Water Intake:

_____

_____.

Today's Supplements Were:

A Characteristic That I Am Choosing To Improve On:

TODAY I WILL PROTECT MY WELLBEING BY

MY LIFESTYLE IS
DIFFERENT BECAUSE
I NOW

THE WEALTH IN MY HEALTH

Today:

Mood:

Today's Physical Goal:

Today I Need:

Today I Am Showing Appreciation To My Body By:

I Will Give Myself What I Need Today By:

Today I Am Choosing To Believe:

I Know I Do Not Need:

Today I Am Replacing An Old Belief With This New Belief (State The New Belief):

Today's Physical Activity Is:

I Will Support My New Beliefs By:

Today I Am Opening Up My Heart And Mind To:

Today's Blood Pressure: _____ Today's Sugar Count: _____

44

Continue To The Next Page

THE WEALTH IN MY HEALTH

For Breakfast Today I Had:

Today's Exercise/Physical Activity Was (State What It Was And For How Long):

For Lunch Today I Had:

Today's Compliment To Myself:

For Dinner Today I Had:

Today I Imagined Myself:

Today I Snacked On:

Although I Wanted To

_____, I

Today's Water Intake:

_____

_____.

Today's Supplements Were:

A Characteristic That I Am Choosing To Improve On:

THE WEALTH IN MY HEALTH

Today: Mood:

Today's Physical Goal: Today I Need:

Today I Am Showing Appreciation To My   I Will Give Myself What I Need Today By:
Body By:

Today I Am Choosing To Believe: I Know I Do Not Need:

Today I Am Replacing An Old Belief With   Today's Physical Activity Is:
This New Belief (State The New Belief):

I Will Support My New Beliefs By: Today I Am Opening Up My Heart And
                                          Mind To:

Today's Blood Pressure: _____ Today's Sugar Count: _____

THE WEALTH IN MY HEALTH
NIGHT ACTIONS AND THOUGHTS

For Breakfast Today I Had:

Today's Exercise/Physical Activity Was (State What It Was And For How Long):

For Lunch Today I Had:

Today's Compliment To Myself:

For Dinner Today I Had:

Today I Imagined Myself:

Today I Snacked On:

Although I Wanted To

_____, I

Today's Water Intake:

_____

_____.

Today's Supplements Were:

A Characteristic That I Am Choosing To Improve On:

WHOLENESS NOTES

I AM HAPPY BECAUSE I AM STARTING TO SEE RESULTS.

THE WEALTH IN MY HEALTH

MORNING ACTIONS AND THOUGHTS

Today:

Mood:

Today's Physical Goal:

Today I Need:

Today I Am Showing Appreciation To My Body By:

I Will Give Myself What I Need Today By:

Today I Am Choosing To Believe:

I Know I Do Not Need:

Today I Am Replacing An Old Belief With This New Belief (State The New Belief):

Today's Physical Activity Is:

I Will Support My New Beliefs By:

Today I Am Opening Up My Heart And Mind To:

Today's Blood Pressure: _____ Today's Sugar Count: _____

Continue To The Next Page

THE WEALTH IN MY HEALTH

For Breakfast Today I Had:

Today's Exercise/Physical Activity Was
(State What It Was And For How Long):

For Lunch Today I Had:

Today's Compliment To Myself:

For Dinner Today I Had:

Today I Imagined Myself:

Today I Snacked On:

Although I Wanted To

_____, I

Today's Water Intake:

_____

_____.

Today's Supplements Were:

A Characteristic That I Am Choosing To
Improve On:

THE WEALTH IN MY HEALTH

MORNING ACTIONS AND THOUGHTS

Today: Mood:

Today's Physical Goal: Today I Need:

Today I Am Showing Appreciation To My   I Will Give Myself What I Need Today By:
Body By:

Today I Am Choosing To Believe: I Know I Do Not Need:

Today I Am Replacing An Old Belief With   Today's Physical Activity Is:
This New Belief (State The New Belief):

I Will Support My New Beliefs By: Today I Am Opening Up My Heart And
                                                Mind To:

Today's Blood Pressure: _____ Today's Sugar Count: _____

THE WEALTH IN MY HEALTH

For Breakfast Today I Had:

Today's Exercise/Physical Activity Was (State What It Was And For How Long):

For Lunch Today I Had:

Today's Compliment To Myself:

For Dinner Today I Had:

Today I Imagined Myself:

Today I Snacked On:

Although I Wanted To

_____, I

Today's Water Intake:

_____

_____.

Today's Supplements Were:

A Characteristic That I Am Choosing To Improve On:

WHOLENESS NOTES

I HAVE CHANGED MY THINKING SO I CAN CHANGE MY EXPERIENCES.

THE WEALTH IN MY HEALTH

Today: Mood:

Today's Physical Goal: Today I Need:

Today I Am Showing Appreciation To My   I Will Give Myself What I Need Today By:
Body By:

Today I Am Choosing To Believe: I Know I Do Not Need:

Today I Am Replacing An Old Belief With   Today's Physical Activity Is:
This New Belief (State The New Belief):

I Will Support My New Beliefs By: Today I Am Opening Up My Heart And
                                                Mind To:

Today's Blood Pressure: _____ Today's Sugar Count: _____

THE WEALTH IN MY HEALTH

For Breakfast Today I Had:

Today's Exercise/Physical Activity Was
(State What It Was And For How Long):

For Lunch Today I Had:

Today's Compliment To Myself:

For Dinner Today I Had:

Today I Imagined Myself:

Today I Snacked On:

Although I Wanted To

_____, I

Today's Water Intake:

_____

_____.

Today's Supplements Were:

A Characteristic That I Am Choosing To
Improve On:

THE WEALTH IN MY HEALTH

Today:

Mood:

Today's Physical Goal:

Today I Need:

Today I Am Showing Appreciation To My Body By:

I Will Give Myself What I Need Today By:

Today I Am Choosing To Believe:

I Know I Do Not Need:

Today I Am Replacing An Old Belief With This New Belief (State The New Belief):

Today's Physical Activity Is:

I Will Support My New Beliefs By:

Today I Am Opening Up My Heart And Mind To:

Today's Blood Pressure: _____ Today's Sugar Count: _____

Continue To The Next Page

THE WEALTH IN MY HEALTH

For Breakfast Today I Had:

For Lunch Today I Had:

For Dinner Today I Had:

Today I Snacked On:

Today's Water Intake:

Today's Supplements Were:

Today's Exercise/Physical Activity Was (State What It Was And For How Long):

Today's Compliment To Myself:

Today I Imagined Myself:

Although I Wanted To

_____, I

_____

_____.

A Characteristic That I Am Choosing To Improve On:

THE WEALTH IN MY HEALTH

Today: Mood:

Today's Physical Goal: Today I Need:

Today I Am Showing Appreciation To My   I Will Give Myself What I Need Today By:
Body By:

Today I Am Choosing To Believe: I Know I Do Not Need:

Today I Am Replacing An Old Belief With   Today's Physical Activity Is:
This New Belief (State The New Belief):

I Will Support My New Beliefs By: Today I Am Opening Up My Heart And
                                              Mind To:

Today's Blood Pressure: _____ Today's Sugar Count: _____

60   Continue To The Next Page

THE WEALTH IN MY HEALTH

For Breakfast Today I Had:

Today's Exercise/Physical Activity Was
(State What It Was And For How Long):

For Lunch Today I Had:

Today's Compliment To Myself:

For Dinner Today I Had:

Today I Imagined Myself:

Today I Snacked On:

Although I Wanted To

_____, I

Today's Water Intake:

_____

_____.

Today's Supplements Were:

A Characteristic That I Am Choosing To
Improve On:

WHOLENESS NOTES

MY FAVORITE THIRTY MINUTE ACTIVITIES ARE

MY PRIORITIES HAVE SHIFTED.

WHOLENESS IS MY PRIORITY.

THE WEALTH IN MY HEALTH

MORNING ACTIONS AND THOUGHTS

Today:

Mood:

Today's Physical Goal:

Today I Need:

Today I Am Showing Appreciation To My Body By:

I Will Give Myself What I Need Today By:

Today I Am Choosing To Believe:

I Know I Do Not Need:

Today I Am Replacing An Old Belief With This New Belief (State The New Belief):

Today's Physical Activity Is:

I Will Support My New Beliefs By:

Today I Am Opening Up My Heart And Mind To:

Today's Blood Pressure: _____ Today's Sugar Count: _____

Continue To The Next Page

THE WEALTH IN MY HEALTH

For Breakfast Today I Had:

Today's Exercise/Physical Activity Was (State What It Was And For How Long):

For Lunch Today I Had:

Today's Compliment To Myself:

For Dinner Today I Had:

Today I Imagined Myself:

Today I Snacked On:

Although I Wanted To

_____, I

Today's Water Intake:

_____

_____.

Today's Supplements Were:

A Characteristic That I Am Choosing To Improve On:

THE WEALTH IN MY HEALTH

Today: Mood:

Today's Physical Goal: Today I Need:

Today I Am Showing Appreciation To My   I Will Give Myself What I Need Today By:
Body By:

Today I Am Choosing To Believe: I Know I Do Not Need:

Today I Am Replacing An Old Belief With   Today's Physical Activity Is:
This New Belief (State The New Belief):

I Will Support My New Beliefs By: Today I Am Opening Up My Heart And
                                                Mind To:

Today's Blood Pressure: _____ Today's Sugar Count: _____

68   Continue To The Next Page

THE WEALTH IN MY HEALTH

For Breakfast Today I Had:

Today's Exercise/Physical Activity Was (State What It Was And For How Long):

For Lunch Today I Had:

Today's Compliment To Myself:

For Dinner Today I Had:

Today I Imagined Myself:

Today I Snacked On:

Although I Wanted To

_____, I

Today's Water Intake:

_____

_____.

Today's Supplements Were:

A Characteristic That I Am Choosing To Improve On:

THE WEALTH IN MY HEALTH

MORNING ACTIONS AND THOUGHTS

Today: Mood:

Today's Physical Goal: Today I Need:

Today I Am Showing Appreciation To My   I Will Give Myself What I Need Today By:
Body By:

Today I Am Choosing To Believe: I Know I Do Not Need:

Today I Am Replacing An Old Belief With   Today's Physical Activity Is:
This New Belief (State The New Belief):

I Will Support My New Beliefs By: Today I Am Opening Up My Heart And
                                                Mind To:

Today's Blood Pressure: _____ Today's Sugar Count: _____

70   Continue To The Next Page

THE WEALTH IN MY HEALTH
NIGHT ACTIONS AND THOUGHTS

For Breakfast Today I Had:

Today's Exercise/Physical Activity Was (State What It Was And For How Long):

For Lunch Today I Had:

Today's Compliment To Myself:

For Dinner Today I Had:

Today I Imagined Myself:

Today I Snacked On:

Although I Wanted To

_____, I

Today's Water Intake:

_____

_____.

Today's Supplements Were:

A Characteristic That I Am Choosing To Improve On:

THE WEALTH IN MY HEALTH

Today: Mood:

Today's Physical Goal: Today I Need:

Today I Am Showing Appreciation To My   I Will Give Myself What I Need Today By:
Body By:

Today I Am Choosing To Believe: I Know I Do Not Need:

Today I Am Replacing An Old Belief With   Today's Physical Activity Is:
This New Belief (State The New Belief):

I Will Support My New Beliefs By: Today I Am Opening Up My Heart And
                                              Mind To:

Today's Blood Pressure: _____ Today's Sugar Count: _____

72   Continue To The Next Page

THE WEALTH IN MY HEALTH

For Breakfast Today I Had:

Today's Exercise/Physical Activity Was (State What It Was And For How Long):

For Lunch Today I Had:

Today's Compliment To Myself:

For Dinner Today I Had:

Today I Imagined Myself:

Today I Snacked On:

Although I Wanted To

_____, I

Today's Water Intake:

_____

_____.

Today's Supplements Were:

A Characteristic That I Am Choosing To Improve On:

THE WEALTH IN MY HEALTH

Today:

Mood:

Today's Physical Goal:

Today I Need:

Today I Am Showing Appreciation To My Body By:

I Will Give Myself What I Need Today By:

Today I Am Choosing To Believe:

I Know I Do Not Need:

Today I Am Replacing An Old Belief With This New Belief (State The New Belief):

Today's Physical Activity Is:

I Will Support My New Beliefs By:

Today I Am Opening Up My Heart And Mind To:

Today's Blood Pressure: _____ Today's Sugar Count: _____

Continue To The Next Page

THE WEALTH IN MY HEALTH

For Breakfast Today I Had:

Today's Exercise/Physical Activity Was
(State What It Was And For How Long):

For Lunch Today I Had:

Today's Compliment To Myself:

For Dinner Today I Had:

Today I Imagined Myself:

Today I Snacked On:

Although I Wanted To

_____, I

Today's Water Intake:

_____

_____.

Today's Supplements Were:

A Characteristic That I Am Choosing To
Improve On:

I EAT TO

WHOLENESS NOTES

THE WEALTH IN MY HEALTH

MORNING ACTIONS AND THOUGHTS

Today: Mood:

Today's Physical Goal: Today I Need:

Today I Am Showing Appreciation To My   I Will Give Myself What I Need Today By:
Body By:

Today I Am Choosing To Believe: I Know I Do Not Need:

Today I Am Replacing An Old Belief With   Today's Physical Activity Is:
This New Belief (State The New Belief):

I Will Support My New Beliefs By: Today I Am Opening Up My Heart And
                                                Mind To:

Today's Blood Pressure: _____ Today's Sugar Count: _____

THE WEALTH IN MY HEALTH

NIGHT ACTIONS AND THOUGHTS

For Breakfast Today I Had:

For Lunch Today I Had:

For Dinner Today I Had:

Today I Snacked On:

Today's Water Intake:

Today's Supplements Were:

Today's Exercise/Physical Activity Was
(State What It Was And For How Long):

Today's Compliment To Myself:

Today I Imagined Myself:

Although I Wanted To

_____, I

_____

_____.

A Characteristic That I Am Choosing To
Improve On:

THE WEALTH IN MY HEALTH

MORNING ACTIONS AND THOUGHTS

Today: Mood:

Today's Physical Goal: Today I Need:

Today I Am Showing Appreciation To My   I Will Give Myself What I Need Today By:
Body By:

Today I Am Choosing To Believe: I Know I Do Not Need:

Today I Am Replacing An Old Belief With   Today's Physical Activity Is:
This New Belief (State The New Belief):

I Will Support My New Beliefs By: Today I Am Opening Up My Heart And
                                                Mind To:

Today's Blood Pressure: _____ Today's Sugar Count: _____

80   Continue To The Next Page

THE WEALTH IN MY HEALTH

NIGHT ACTIONS AND THOUGHTS

For Breakfast Today I Had:

Today's Exercise/Physical Activity Was
(State What It Was And For How Long):

For Lunch Today I Had:

Today's Compliment To Myself:

For Dinner Today I Had:

Today I Imagined Myself:

Today I Snacked On:

Although I Wanted To

_____, I

Today's Water Intake:

_____

_____.

Today's Supplements Were:

A Characteristic That I Am Choosing To
Improve On:

THE WEALTH IN MY HEALTH

MORNING ACTIONS AND THOUGHTS

Today: Mood:

Today's Physical Goal: Today I Need:

Today I Am Showing Appreciation To My   I Will Give Myself What I Need Today By:
Body By:

Today I Am Choosing To Believe: I Know I Do Not Need:

Today I Am Replacing An Old Belief With   Today's Physical Activity Is:
This New Belief (State The New Belief):

I Will Support My New Beliefs By: Today I Am Opening Up My Heart And
                                          Mind To:

Today's Blood Pressure: _____ Today's Sugar Count: _____

82   Continue To The Next Page

THE WEALTH IN MY HEALTH
NIGHT ACTIONS AND THOUGHTS

For Breakfast Today I Had:

Today's Exercise/Physical Activity Was (State What It Was And For How Long):

For Lunch Today I Had:

Today's Compliment To Myself:

For Dinner Today I Had:

Today I Imagined Myself:

Today I Snacked On:

Although I Wanted To

_____, I

Today's Water Intake:

_____

_____.

Today's Supplements Were:

A Characteristic That I Am Choosing To Improve On:

MY NEXT LEVEL REQUIRES A DIFFERENT ME.

THE WAY I EAT HAS CHANGED. I HAVE SUBTRACTED THESE FOODS AND ADDED THESE FOODS

THE WEALTH IN MY HEALTH

MORNING ACTIONS AND THOUGHTS

Today:

Mood:

Today's Physical Goal:

Today I Need:

Today I Am Showing Appreciation To My Body By:

I Will Give Myself What I Need Today By:

Today I Am Choosing To Believe:

I Know I Do Not Need:

Today I Am Replacing An Old Belief With This New Belief (State The New Belief):

Today's Physical Activity Is:

I Will Support My New Beliefs By:

Today I Am Opening Up My Heart And Mind To:

Today's Blood Pressure: _____ Today's Sugar Count: _____

86

Continue To The Next Page

THE WEALTH IN MY HEALTH

For Breakfast Today I Had:

Today's Exercise/Physical Activity Was (State What It Was And For How Long):

For Lunch Today I Had:

Today's Compliment To Myself:

For Dinner Today I Had:

Today I Imagined Myself:

Today I Snacked On:

Although I Wanted To

_____, I

Today's Water Intake:

_____

_____.

Today's Supplements Were:

A Characteristic That I Am Choosing To Improve On:

THE WEALTH IN MY HEALTH

MORNING ACTIONS AND THOUGHTS

Today:

Mood:

Today's Physical Goal:

Today I Need:

Today I Am Showing Appreciation To My Body By:

I Will Give Myself What I Need Today By:

Today I Am Choosing To Believe:

I Know I Do Not Need:

Today I Am Replacing An Old Belief With This New Belief (State The New Belief):

Today's Physical Activity Is:

I Will Support My New Beliefs By:

Today I Am Opening Up My Heart And Mind To:

Today's Blood Pressure: _____ Today's Sugar Count: _____

Continue To The Next Page

THE WEALTH IN MY HEALTH

For Breakfast Today I Had:

Today's Exercise/Physical Activity Was (State What It Was And For How Long):

For Lunch Today I Had:

Today's Compliment To Myself:

For Dinner Today I Had:

Today I Imagined Myself:

Today I Snacked On:

Although I Wanted To

_____, I

Today's Water Intake:

_____

_____.

Today's Supplements Were:

A Characteristic That I Am Choosing To Improve On:

THE WEALTH IN MY HEALTH

MORNING ACTIONS AND THOUGHTS

Today:

Mood:

Today's Physical Goal:

Today I Need:

Today I Am Showing Appreciation To My Body By:

I Will Give Myself What I Need Today By:

Today I Am Choosing To Believe:

I Know I Do Not Need:

Today I Am Replacing An Old Belief With This New Belief (State The New Belief):

Today's Physical Activity Is:

I Will Support My New Beliefs By:

Today I Am Opening Up My Heart And Mind To:

Today's Blood Pressure: _____ Today's Sugar Count: _____

90

Continue To The Next Page

THE WEALTH IN MY HEALTH

For Breakfast Today I Had:

Today's Exercise/Physical Activity Was (State What It Was And For How Long):

For Lunch Today I Had:

Today's Compliment To Myself:

For Dinner Today I Had:

Today I Imagined Myself:

Today I Snacked On:

Although I Wanted To

_____, I

Today's Water Intake:

_____

_____.

Today's Supplements Were:

A Characteristic That I Am Choosing To Improve On:

THE WEALTH IN MY HEALTH

Today:

Mood:

Today's Physical Goal:

Today I Need:

Today I Am Showing Appreciation To My Body By:

I Will Give Myself What I Need Today By:

Today I Am Choosing To Believe:

I Know I Do Not Need:

Today I Am Replacing An Old Belief With This New Belief (State The New Belief):

Today's Physical Activity Is:

I Will Support My New Beliefs By:

Today I Am Opening Up My Heart And Mind To:

Today's Blood Pressure: _____ Today's Sugar Count: _____

Continue To The Next Page

THE WEALTH IN MY HEALTH

For Breakfast Today I Had:

Today's Exercise/Physical Activity Was (State What It Was And For How Long):

For Lunch Today I Had:

Today's Compliment To Myself:

For Dinner Today I Had:

Today I Imagined Myself:

Today I Snacked On:

Although I Wanted To

_____, I

Today's Water Intake:

_____

_____.

Today's Supplements Were:

A Characteristic That I Am Choosing To Improve On:

NO LONGER AM I STUCK. I'M DOING SOMETHING ABOUT IT. I'M DOING BETTER.

WHOLENESS NOTES

THE WEALTH IN MY HEALTH

MORNING ACTIONS AND THOUGHTS

Today:

Mood:

Today's Physical Goal:

Today I Need:

Today I Am Showing Appreciation To My Body By:

I Will Give Myself What I Need Today By:

Today I Am Choosing To Believe:

I Know I Do Not Need:

Today I Am Replacing An Old Belief With This New Belief (State The New Belief):

Today's Physical Activity Is:

I Will Support My New Beliefs By:

Today I Am Opening Up My Heart And Mind To:

Today's Blood Pressure: _____ Today's Sugar Count: _____

THE WEALTH IN MY HEALTH

For Breakfast Today I Had:

Today's Exercise/Physical Activity Was
(State What It Was And For How Long):

For Lunch Today I Had:

Today's Compliment To Myself:

For Dinner Today I Had:

Today I Imagined Myself:

Today I Snacked On:

Although I Wanted To

_____, I

Today's Water Intake:

_____

_____.

Today's Supplements Were:

A Characteristic That I Am Choosing To
Improve On:

THE WEALTH IN MY HEALTH

Today:

Mood:

Today's Physical Goal:

Today I Need:

Today I Am Showing Appreciation To My Body By:

I Will Give Myself What I Need Today By:

Today I Am Choosing To Believe:

I Know I Do Not Need:

Today I Am Replacing An Old Belief With This New Belief (State The New Belief):

Today's Physical Activity Is:

I Will Support My New Beliefs By:

Today I Am Opening Up My Heart And Mind To:

Today's Blood Pressure: _____ Today's Sugar Count: _____

Continue To The Next Page

THE WEALTH IN MY HEALTH

For Breakfast Today I Had:

Today's Exercise/Physical Activity Was (State What It Was And For How Long):

For Lunch Today I Had:

Today's Compliment To Myself:

For Dinner Today I Had:

Today I Imagined Myself:

Today I Snacked On:

Although I Wanted To

_____, I

Today's Water Intake:

_____

_____.

Today's Supplements Were:

A Characteristic That I Am Choosing To Improve On:

I AM
GOING TO MAKE
YOU SO PROUD.
I AM GOING
TO MAKE YOU
STRONG.
- SAYS SELF

I AM HAPPY BECAUSE I KEEP GOING.

THE WEALTH IN MY HEALTH
MORNING ACTIONS AND THOUGHTS

Today: Mood:

Today's Physical Goal: Today I Need:

Today I Am Showing Appreciation To My   I Will Give Myself What I Need Today By:
Body By:

Today I Am Choosing To Believe: I Know I Do Not Need:

Today I Am Replacing An Old Belief With   Today's Physical Activity Is:
This New Belief (State The New Belief):

I Will Support My New Beliefs By: Today I Am Opening Up My Heart And
                                                 Mind To:

Today's Blood Pressure: _____ Today's Sugar Count: _____

THE WEALTH IN MY HEALTH

For Breakfast Today I Had:

Today's Exercise/Physical Activity Was (State What It Was And For How Long):

For Lunch Today I Had:

Today's Compliment To Myself:

For Dinner Today I Had:

Today I Imagined Myself:

Today I Snacked On:

Although I Wanted To

_____, I

Today's Water Intake:

_____

_____.

Today's Supplements Were:

A Characteristic That I Am Choosing To Improve On:

I HAVE
ACCEPTED MY

WHOLENESS NOTES

THE WEALTH IN MY HEALTH

Today:

Mood:

Today's Physical Goal:

Today I Need:

Today I Am Showing Appreciation To My Body By:

I Will Give Myself What I Need Today By:

Today I Am Choosing To Believe:

I Know I Do Not Need:

Today I Am Replacing An Old Belief With This New Belief (State The New Belief):

Today's Physical Activity Is:

I Will Support My New Beliefs By:

Today I Am Opening Up My Heart And Mind To:

Today's Blood Pressure: _____ Today's Sugar Count: _____

106

Continue To The Next Page

THE WEALTH IN MY HEALTH

For Breakfast Today I Had:

Today's Exercise/Physical Activity Was
(State What It Was And For How Long):

For Lunch Today I Had:

Today's Compliment To Myself:

For Dinner Today I Had:

Today I Imagined Myself:

Today I Snacked On:

Although I Wanted To

_____, I

Today's Water Intake:

_____

_____.

Today's Supplements Were:

A Characteristic That I Am Choosing To
Improve On:

THE WEALTH IN MY HEALTH

Today: Mood:

Today's Physical Goal: Today I Need:

Today I Am Showing Appreciation To My   I Will Give Myself What I Need Today By:
Body By:

Today I Am Choosing To Believe: I Know I Do Not Need:

Today I Am Replacing An Old Belief With   Today's Physical Activity Is:
This New Belief (State The New Belief):

I Will Support My New Beliefs By: Today I Am Opening Up My Heart And
                                          Mind To:

Today's Blood Pressure: _____ Today's Sugar Count: _____

108   Continue To The Next Page

THE WEALTH IN MY HEALTH

For Breakfast Today I Had:

Today's Exercise/Physical Activity Was (State What It Was And For How Long):

For Lunch Today I Had:

Today's Compliment To Myself:

For Dinner Today I Had:

Today I Imagined Myself:

Today I Snacked On:

Although I Wanted To

_____, I

Today's Water Intake:

_____

_____.

Today's Supplements Were:

A Characteristic That I Am Choosing To Improve On:

THE WEALTH IN MY HEALTH

Today: Mood:

Today's Physical Goal: Today I Need:

Today I Am Showing Appreciation To My   I Will Give Myself What I Need Today By:
Body By:

Today I Am Choosing To Believe: I Know I Do Not Need:

Today I Am Replacing An Old Belief With   Today's Physical Activity Is:
This New Belief (State The New Belief):

I Will Support My New Beliefs By: Today I Am Opening Up My Heart And
                                          Mind To:

Today's Blood Pressure: _____ Today's Sugar Count: _____

THE WEALTH IN MY HEALTH

For Breakfast Today I Had:

Today's Exercise/Physical Activity Was (State What It Was And For How Long):

For Lunch Today I Had:

Today's Compliment To Myself:

For Dinner Today I Had:

Today I Imagined Myself:

Today I Snacked On:

Although I Wanted To

_____, I

Today's Water Intake:

_____

_____.

Today's Supplements Were:

A Characteristic That I Am Choosing To Improve On:

WHAT IT TAKES FOR ME TO BE HAPPY

WHOLENESS NOTES

THE WEALTH IN MY HEALTH

Today: Mood:

Today's Physical Goal: Today I Need:

Today I Am Showing Appreciation To My   I Will Give Myself What I Need Today By:
Body By:

Today I Am Choosing To Believe: I Know I Do Not Need:

Today I Am Replacing An Old Belief With   Today's Physical Activity Is:
This New Belief (State The New Belief):

I Will Support My New Beliefs By: Today I Am Opening Up My Heart And
                                                Mind To:

Today's Blood Pressure: _____ Today's Sugar Count: _____

114   Continue To The Next Page

THE WEALTH IN MY HEALTH

For Breakfast Today I Had:

Today's Exercise/Physical Activity Was (State What It Was And For How Long):

For Lunch Today I Had:

Today's Compliment To Myself:

For Dinner Today I Had:

Today I Imagined Myself:

Today I Snacked On:

Although I Wanted To

_____, I

Today's Water Intake:

_____

_____.

Today's Supplements Were:

A Characteristic That I Am Choosing To Improve On:

THE WEALTH IN MY HEALTH

Today: Mood:

Today's Physical Goal: Today I Need:

Today I Am Showing Appreciation To My   I Will Give Myself What I Need Today By:
Body By:

Today I Am Choosing To Believe: I Know I Do Not Need:

Today I Am Replacing An Old Belief With   Today's Physical Activity Is:
This New Belief (State The New Belief):

I Will Support My New Beliefs By: Today I Am Opening Up My Heart And
                                                     Mind To:

Today's Blood Pressure: _____ Today's Sugar Count: _____

116   Continue To The Next Page

THE WEALTH IN MY HEALTH

For Breakfast Today I Had:

Today's Exercise/Physical Activity Was (State What It Was And For How Long):

For Lunch Today I Had:

Today's Compliment To Myself:

For Dinner Today I Had:

Today I Imagined Myself:

Today I Snacked On:

Although I Wanted To

_____, I

Today's Water Intake:

_____

_____.

Today's Supplements Were:

A Characteristic That I Am Choosing To Improve On:

THE WEALTH IN MY HEALTH

Today: Mood:

Today's Physical Goal: Today I Need:

Today I Am Showing Appreciation To My   I Will Give Myself What I Need Today By:
Body By:

Today I Am Choosing To Believe: I Know I Do Not Need:

Today I Am Replacing An Old Belief With   Today's Physical Activity Is:
This New Belief (State The New Belief):

I Will Support My New Beliefs By: Today I Am Opening Up My Heart And
                                                Mind To:

Today's Blood Pressure: _____ Today's Sugar Count: _____

118   Continue To The Next Page

THE WEALTH IN MY HEALTH

For Breakfast Today I Had:

Today's Exercise/Physical Activity Was
(State What It Was And For How Long):

For Lunch Today I Had:

Today's Compliment To Myself:

For Dinner Today I Had:

Today I Imagined Myself:

Today I Snacked On:

Although I Wanted To

_____, I

Today's Water Intake:

_____

_____.

Today's Supplements Were:

A Characteristic That I Am Choosing To
Improve On:

MY IDENTITY IS ATTACHED TO

NO MORE...

THE WEALTH IN MY HEALTH

Today:

Mood:

Today's Physical Goal:

Today I Need:

Today I Am Showing Appreciation To My Body By:

I Will Give Myself What I Need Today By:

Today I Am Choosing To Believe:

I Know I Do Not Need:

Today I Am Replacing An Old Belief With This New Belief (State The New Belief):

Today's Physical Activity Is:

I Will Support My New Beliefs By:

Today I Am Opening Up My Heart And Mind To:

Today's Blood Pressure: _____ Today's Sugar Count: _____

122

Continue To The Next Page

THE WEALTH IN MY HEALTH

For Breakfast Today I Had:

Today's Exercise/Physical Activity Was
(State What It Was And For How Long):

For Lunch Today I Had:

Today's Compliment To Myself:

For Dinner Today I Had:

Today I Imagined Myself:

Today I Snacked On:

Although I Wanted To

_____, I

Today's Water Intake:

_____

_____.

Today's Supplements Were:

A Characteristic That I Am Choosing To
Improve On:

THE WEALTH IN MY HEALTH

Today: Mood:

Today's Physical Goal: Today I Need:

Today I Am Showing Appreciation To My   I Will Give Myself What I Need Today By:
Body By:

Today I Am Choosing To Believe: I Know I Do Not Need:

Today I Am Replacing An Old Belief With   Today's Physical Activity Is:
This New Belief (State The New Belief):

I Will Support My New Beliefs By: Today I Am Opening Up My Heart And
                                                Mind To:

Today's Blood Pressure: _____ Today's Sugar Count: _____

124   Continue To The Next Page

THE WEALTH IN MY HEALTH

For Breakfast Today I Had:

Today's Exercise/Physical Activity Was (State What It Was And For How Long):

For Lunch Today I Had:

Today's Compliment To Myself:

For Dinner Today I Had:

Today I Imagined Myself:

Today I Snacked On:

Although I Wanted To

_____, I

Today's Water Intake:

_____

_____.

Today's Supplements Were:

A Characteristic That I Am Choosing To Improve On:

THE WEALTH IN MY HEALTH

Today:

Mood:

Today's Physical Goal:

Today I Need:

Today I Am Showing Appreciation To My Body By:

I Will Give Myself What I Need Today By:

Today I Am Choosing To Believe:

I Know I Do Not Need:

Today I Am Replacing An Old Belief With This New Belief (State The New Belief):

Today's Physical Activity Is:

I Will Support My New Beliefs By:

Today I Am Opening Up My Heart And Mind To:

Today's Blood Pressure: _____ Today's Sugar Count: _____

126

Continue To The Next Page

THE WEALTH IN MY HEALTH
NIGHT ACTIONS AND THOUGHTS

For Breakfast Today I Had:

Today's Exercise/Physical Activity Was (State What It Was And For How Long):

For Lunch Today I Had:

Today's Compliment To Myself:

For Dinner Today I Had:

Today I Imagined Myself:

Today I Snacked On:

Although I Wanted To

_____, I

Today's Water Intake:

_____

_____.

Today's Supplements Were:

A Characteristic That I Am Choosing To Improve On:

I'M MAKING SPACE FOR IMPROVEMENT. NO MATTER HOW MUCH IT HURTS.

I AM PERFECT AND WHOLE JUST THE WAY I AM.

FOR ME, THE DIFFERENCE BETWEEN HAPPINESS AND FULFILLMENT IS

WHOLENESS NOTES

THE WEALTH IN MY HEALTH

Today: Mood:

Today's Physical Goal: Today I Need:

Today I Am Showing Appreciation To My   I Will Give Myself What I Need Today By:
Body By:

Today I Am Choosing To Believe: I Know I Do Not Need:

Today I Am Replacing An Old Belief With   Today's Physical Activity Is:
This New Belief (State The New Belief):

I Will Support My New Beliefs By: Today I Am Opening Up My Heart And
                                          Mind To:

Today's Blood Pressure: _____ Today's Sugar Count: _____

132   Continue To The Next Page

THE WEALTH IN MY HEALTH

For Breakfast Today I Had:

Today's Exercise/Physical Activity Was (State What It Was And For How Long):

For Lunch Today I Had:

Today's Compliment To Myself:

For Dinner Today I Had:

Today I Imagined Myself:

Today I Snacked On:

Although I Wanted To

_____, I

Today's Water Intake:

_____

_____.

Today's Supplements Were:

A Characteristic That I Am Choosing To Improve On:

THE WEALTH IN MY HEALTH

MORNING ACTIONS AND THOUGHTS

Today:

Mood:

Today's Physical Goal:

Today I Need:

Today I Am Showing Appreciation To My Body By:

I Will Give Myself What I Need Today By:

Today I Am Choosing To Believe:

I Know I Do Not Need:

Today I Am Replacing An Old Belief With This New Belief (State The New Belief):

Today's Physical Activity Is:

I Will Support My New Beliefs By:

Today I Am Opening Up My Heart And Mind To:

Today's Blood Pressure: _____ Today's Sugar Count: _____

Continue To The Next Page

THE WEALTH IN MY HEALTH

For Breakfast Today I Had:

Today's Exercise/Physical Activity Was
(State What It Was And For How Long):

For Lunch Today I Had:

Today's Compliment To Myself:

For Dinner Today I Had:

Today I Imagined Myself:

Today I Snacked On:

Although I Wanted To

_____, I

Today's Water Intake:

_____

_____.

Today's Supplements Were:

A Characteristic That I Am Choosing To
Improve On:

THE WEALTH IN MY HEALTH

MORNING ACTIONS AND THOUGHTS

Today: Mood:

Today's Physical Goal: Today I Need:

Today I Am Showing Appreciation To My   I Will Give Myself What I Need Today By:
Body By:

Today I Am Choosing To Believe: I Know I Do Not Need:

Today I Am Replacing An Old Belief With   Today's Physical Activity Is:
This New Belief (State The New Belief):

I Will Support My New Beliefs By: Today I Am Opening Up My Heart And
                                          Mind To:

Today's Blood Pressure: _____ Today's Sugar Count: _____

                                    Continue To The Next Page

THE WEALTH IN MY HEALTH

For Breakfast Today I Had:

Today's Exercise/Physical Activity Was
(State What It Was And For How Long):

For Lunch Today I Had:

Today's Compliment To Myself:

For Dinner Today I Had:

Today I Imagined Myself:

Today I Snacked On:

Although I Wanted To

_____, I

Today's Water Intake:

_____

_____.

Today's Supplements Were:

A Characteristic That I Am Choosing To
Improve On:

WHOLENESS NOTES

EATING HEALTHY WILL CHANGE MY LIFE BY

THE WEALTH IN MY HEALTH

Today: Mood:

Today's Physical Goal: Today I Need:

Today I Am Showing Appreciation To My   I Will Give Myself What I Need Today By:
Body By:

Today I Am Choosing To Believe: I Know I Do Not Need:

Today I Am Replacing An Old Belief With   Today's Physical Activity Is:
This New Belief (State The New Belief):

I Will Support My New Beliefs By: Today I Am Opening Up My Heart And
                                                Mind To:

Today's Blood Pressure: _____ Today's Sugar Count: _____

140   Continue To The Next Page

THE WEALTH IN MY HEALTH

For Breakfast Today I Had:

Today's Exercise/Physical Activity Was (State What It Was And For How Long):

For Lunch Today I Had:

Today's Compliment To Myself:

For Dinner Today I Had:

Today I Imagined Myself:

Today I Snacked On:

Although I Wanted To

_____, I

Today's Water Intake:

_____

_____.

Today's Supplements Were:

A Characteristic That I Am Choosing To Improve On:

THE WEALTH IN MY HEALTH

MORNING ACTIONS AND THOUGHTS

Today:

Mood:

Today's Physical Goal:

Today I Need:

Today I Am Showing Appreciation To My Body By:

I Will Give Myself What I Need Today By:

Today I Am Choosing To Believe:

I Know I Do Not Need:

Today I Am Replacing An Old Belief With This New Belief (State The New Belief):

Today's Physical Activity Is:

I Will Support My New Beliefs By:

Today I Am Opening Up My Heart And Mind To:

Today's Blood Pressure: _____ Today's Sugar Count: _____

142

Continue To The Next Page

THE WEALTH IN MY HEALTH

For Breakfast Today I Had:

Today's Exercise/Physical Activity Was (State What It Was And For How Long):

For Lunch Today I Had:

Today's Compliment To Myself:

For Dinner Today I Had:

Today I Imagined Myself:

Today I Snacked On:

Although I Wanted To

_____, I

Today's Water Intake:

_____

_____.

Today's Supplements Were:

A Characteristic That I Am Choosing To Improve On:

Affirmation #38: I Am Highly Motivated. My Actions Motivate Others.

143

THE WEALTH IN MY HEALTH

Today: Mood:

Today's Physical Goal: Today I Need:

Today I Am Showing Appreciation To My   I Will Give Myself What I Need Today By:
Body By:

Today I Am Choosing To Believe: I Know I Do Not Need:

Today I Am Replacing An Old Belief With   Today's Physical Activity Is:
This New Belief (State The New Belief):

I Will Support My New Beliefs By: Today I Am Opening Up My Heart And
                                          Mind To:

Today's Blood Pressure: _____ Today's Sugar Count: _____

144   Continue To The Next Page

THE WEALTH IN MY HEALTH

For Breakfast Today I Had:

Today's Exercise/Physical Activity Was (State What It Was And For How Long):

For Lunch Today I Had:

Today's Compliment To Myself:

For Dinner Today I Had:

Today I Imagined Myself:

Today I Snacked On:

Although I Wanted To

_____, I

Today's Water Intake:

_____

_____.

Today's Supplements Were:

A Characteristic That I Am Choosing To Improve On:

MY MIND, BODY AND SPIRIT HAVE NOW BECOME MY BEST FRIENDS.

I HAVE GIVEN UP BEFORE. IT WON'T HAPPEN AGAIN.

THE WEALTH IN MY HEALTH

Today:

Mood:

Today's Physical Goal:

Today I Need:

Today I Am Showing Appreciation To My Body By:

I Will Give Myself What I Need Today By:

Today I Am Choosing To Believe:

I Know I Do Not Need:

Today I Am Replacing An Old Belief With This New Belief (State The New Belief):

Today's Physical Activity Is:

I Will Support My New Beliefs By:

Today I Am Opening Up My Heart And Mind To:

Today's Blood Pressure: _____ Today's Sugar Count: _____

148

Continue To The Next Page

THE WEALTH IN MY HEALTH

For Breakfast Today I Had:

Today's Exercise/Physical Activity Was
(State What It Was And For How Long):

For Lunch Today I Had:

Today's Compliment To Myself:

For Dinner Today I Had:

Today I Imagined Myself:

Today I Snacked On:

Although I Wanted To

_____, I

Today's Water Intake:

_____

_____.

Today's Supplements Were:

A Characteristic That I Am Choosing To
Improve On:

I STOPPED ALLOWING FAKE THINGS TO ENTER MY MIND, BODY & SPIRIT.

WHOLENESS NOTES

THE WEALTH IN MY HEALTH

Today: Mood:

Today's Physical Goal: Today I Need:

Today I Am Showing Appreciation To My   I Will Give Myself What I Need Today By:
Body By:

Today I Am Choosing To Believe: I Know I Do Not Need:

Today I Am Replacing An Old Belief With   Today's Physical Activity Is:
This New Belief (State The New Belief):

I Will Support My New Beliefs By: Today I Am Opening Up My Heart And
                                              Mind To:

Today's Blood Pressure: _____ Today's Sugar Count: _____

152   Continue To The Next Page

THE WEALTH IN MY HEALTH

For Breakfast Today I Had:

Today's Exercise/Physical Activity Was (State What It Was And For How Long):

For Lunch Today I Had:

Today's Compliment To Myself:

For Dinner Today I Had:

Today I Imagined Myself:

Today I Snacked On:

Although I Wanted To

_____, I

Today's Water Intake:

_____

_____.

Today's Supplements Were:

A Characteristic That I Am Choosing To Improve On:

THE WEALTH IN MY HEALTH

MORNING ACTIONS AND THOUGHTS

Today: Mood:

Today's Physical Goal: Today I Need:

Today I Am Showing Appreciation To My Body By: I Will Give Myself What I Need Today By:

Today I Am Choosing To Believe: I Know I Do Not Need:

Today I Am Replacing An Old Belief With This New Belief (State The New Belief):   Today's Physical Activity Is:

I Will Support My New Beliefs By: Today I Am Opening Up My Heart And Mind To:

Today's Blood Pressure: _____ Today's Sugar Count: _____

154   Continue To The Next Page

THE WEALTH IN MY HEALTH

For Breakfast Today I Had:

Today's Exercise/Physical Activity Was
(State What It Was And For How Long):

For Lunch Today I Had:

Today's Compliment To Myself:

For Dinner Today I Had:

Today I Imagined Myself:

Today I Snacked On:

Although I Wanted To

_____, I

Today's Water Intake:

_____

_____.

Today's Supplements Were:

A Characteristic That I Am Choosing To
Improve On:

I USE MY STRENGTHS TO

MY FAVORITE PEOPLE TO CALL TO HELP CHANGE MY MOOD

THE WEALTH IN MY HEALTH

Today:

Mood:

Today's Physical Goal:

Today I Need:

Today I Am Showing Appreciation To My Body By:

I Will Give Myself What I Need Today By:

Today I Am Choosing To Believe:

I Know I Do Not Need:

Today I Am Replacing An Old Belief With This New Belief (State The New Belief):

Today's Physical Activity Is:

I Will Support My New Beliefs By:

Today I Am Opening Up My Heart And Mind To:

Today's Blood Pressure: _____ Today's Sugar Count: _____

158

Continue To The Next Page

THE WEALTH IN MY HEALTH

For Breakfast Today I Had:

For Lunch Today I Had:

For Dinner Today I Had:

Today I Snacked On:

Today's Water Intake:

Today's Supplements Were:

Today's Exercise/Physical Activity Was (State What It Was And For How Long):

Today's Compliment To Myself:

Today I Imagined Myself:

Although I Wanted To

_____, I

_____

_____.

A Characteristic That I Am Choosing To Improve On:

THE WEALTH IN MY HEALTH

Today:

Mood:

Today's Physical Goal:

Today I Need:

Today I Am Showing Appreciation To My Body By:

I Will Give Myself What I Need Today By:

Today I Am Choosing To Believe:

I Know I Do Not Need:

Today I Am Replacing An Old Belief With This New Belief (State The New Belief):

Today's Physical Activity Is:

I Will Support My New Beliefs By:

Today I Am Opening Up My Heart And Mind To:

Today's Blood Pressure: _____ Today's Sugar Count: _____

Continue To The Next Page

THE WEALTH IN MY HEALTH

For Breakfast Today I Had:

Today's Exercise/Physical Activity Was (State What It Was And For How Long):

For Lunch Today I Had:

Today's Compliment To Myself:

For Dinner Today I Had:

Today I Imagined Myself:

Today I Snacked On:

Although I Wanted To

_____, I

Today's Water Intake:

_____

_____.

Today's Supplements Were:

A Characteristic That I Am Choosing To Improve On:

WHEN I EAT JUNK FOOD I FEEL

WHOLENESS NOTES

THE WEALTH IN MY HEALTH

MORNING ACTIONS AND THOUGHTS

Today: Mood:

Today's Physical Goal: Today I Need:

Today I Am Showing Appreciation To My   I Will Give Myself What I Need Today By:
Body By:

Today I Am Choosing To Believe: I Know I Do Not Need:

Today I Am Replacing An Old Belief With   Today's Physical Activity Is:
This New Belief (State The New Belief):

I Will Support My New Beliefs By: Today I Am Opening Up My Heart And
                                                Mind To:

Today's Blood Pressure: _____ Today's Sugar Count: _____

164   Continue To The Next Page

THE WEALTH IN MY HEALTH

For Breakfast Today I Had:

Today's Exercise/Physical Activity Was (State What It Was And For How Long):

For Lunch Today I Had:

Today's Compliment To Myself:

For Dinner Today I Had:

Today I Imagined Myself:

Today I Snacked On:

Although I Wanted To

_____, I

Today's Water Intake:

_____

_____.

Today's Supplements Were:

A Characteristic That I Am Choosing To Improve On:

THE WEALTH IN MY HEALTH

MORNING ACTIONS AND THOUGHTS

Today: Mood:

Today's Physical Goal: Today I Need:

Today I Am Showing Appreciation To My Body By: I Will Give Myself What I Need Today By:

Today I Am Choosing To Believe: I Know I Do Not Need:

Today I Am Replacing An Old Belief With This New Belief (State The New Belief):   Today's Physical Activity Is:

I Will Support My New Beliefs By: Today I Am Opening Up My Heart And Mind To:

Today's Blood Pressure: _____ Today's Sugar Count: _____

166   Continue To The Next Page

THE WEALTH IN MY HEALTH

For Breakfast Today I Had:

For Lunch Today I Had:

For Dinner Today I Had:

Today I Snacked On:

Today's Water Intake:

Today's Supplements Were:

Today's Exercise/Physical Activity Was (State What It Was And For How Long):

Today's Compliment To Myself:

Today I Imagined Myself:

Although I Wanted To

_____, I

_____

_____.

A Characteristic That I Am Choosing To Improve On:

THE WEALTH IN MY HEALTH

Today: Mood:

Today's Physical Goal: Today I Need:

Today I Am Showing Appreciation To My   I Will Give Myself What I Need Today By:
Body By:

Today I Am Choosing To Believe: I Know I Do Not Need:

Today I Am Replacing An Old Belief With   Today's Physical Activity Is:
This New Belief (State The New Belief):

I Will Support My New Beliefs By: Today I Am Opening Up My Heart And
                                           Mind To:

Today's Blood Pressure: _____ Today's Sugar Count: _____

168   Continue To The Next Page

THE WEALTH IN MY HEALTH

For Breakfast Today I Had:

Today's Exercise/Physical Activity Was (State What It Was And For How Long):

For Lunch Today I Had:

Today's Compliment To Myself:

For Dinner Today I Had:

Today I Imagined Myself:

Today I Snacked On:

Although I Wanted To

_____, I

Today's Water Intake:

_____

_____.

Today's Supplements Were:

A Characteristic That I Am Choosing To Improve On:

WHOLENESS NOTES

SEVEN EXPERIENCES I HAVE VALUED OVER MY POSSESSIONS ARE

THE WEALTH IN MY HEALTH

Today:

Mood:

Today's Physical Goal:

Today I Need:

Today I Am Showing Appreciation To My Body By:

I Will Give Myself What I Need Today By:

Today I Am Choosing To Believe:

I Know I Do Not Need:

Today I Am Replacing An Old Belief With This New Belief (State The New Belief):

Today's Physical Activity Is:

I Will Support My New Beliefs By:

Today I Am Opening Up My Heart And Mind To:

Today's Blood Pressure: _____ Today's Sugar Count: _____

THE WEALTH IN MY HEALTH

For Breakfast Today I Had:

Today's Exercise/Physical Activity Was (State What It Was And For How Long):

For Lunch Today I Had:

Today's Compliment To Myself:

For Dinner Today I Had:

Today I Imagined Myself:

Today I Snacked On:

Although I Wanted To

_____, I

Today's Water Intake:

_____

_____.

Today's Supplements Were:

A Characteristic That I Am Choosing To Improve On:

THE WEALTH IN MY HEALTH

MORNING ACTIONS AND THOUGHTS

Today:

Mood:

Today's Physical Goal:

Today I Need:

Today I Am Showing Appreciation To My Body By:

I Will Give Myself What I Need Today By:

Today I Am Choosing To Believe:

I Know I Do Not Need:

Today I Am Replacing An Old Belief With This New Belief (State The New Belief):

Today's Physical Activity Is:

I Will Support My New Beliefs By:

Today I Am Opening Up My Heart And Mind To:

Today's Blood Pressure: _____ Today's Sugar Count: _____

174

Continue To The Next Page

THE WEALTH IN MY HEALTH
NIGHT ACTIONS AND THOUGHTS

For Breakfast Today I Had:

Today's Exercise/Physical Activity Was
(State What It Was And For How Long):

For Lunch Today I Had:

Today's Compliment To Myself:

For Dinner Today I Had:

Today I Imagined Myself:

Today I Snacked On:

Although I Wanted To

_____, I

Today's Water Intake:

_____

_____.

Today's Supplements Were:

A Characteristic That I Am Choosing To
Improve On:

THE WEALTH IN MY HEALTH

MORNING ACTIONS AND THOUGHTS

Today:

Mood:

Today's Physical Goal:

Today I Need:

Today I Am Showing Appreciation To My Body By:

I Will Give Myself What I Need Today By:

Today I Am Choosing To Believe:

I Know I Do Not Need:

Today I Am Replacing An Old Belief With This New Belief (State The New Belief):

Today's Physical Activity Is:

I Will Support My New Beliefs By:

Today I Am Opening Up My Heart And Mind To:

Today's Blood Pressure: _____ Today's Sugar Count: _____

Continue To The Next Page

THE WEALTH IN MY HEALTH

For Breakfast Today I Had:

For Lunch Today I Had:

For Dinner Today I Had:

Today I Snacked On:

Today's Water Intake:

Today's Supplements Were:

Today's Exercise/Physical Activity Was
(State What It Was And For How Long):

Today's Compliment To Myself:

Today I Imagined Myself:

Although I Wanted To

_____, I

_____

_____.

A Characteristic That I Am Choosing To
Improve On:

I PICTURE MYSELF

THEY WANT ME TO CHANGE JUST A LITTLE, BUT I'M CHANGING A WHOLE LOT. IT FEELS GOOD.

THE WEALTH IN MY HEALTH

MORNING ACTIONS AND THOUGHTS

Today: Mood:

Today's Physical Goal: Today I Need:

Today I Am Showing Appreciation To My   I Will Give Myself What I Need Today By:
Body By:

Today I Am Choosing To Believe: I Know I Do Not Need:

Today I Am Replacing An Old Belief With   Today's Physical Activity Is:
This New Belief (State The New Belief):

I Will Support My New Beliefs By: Today I Am Opening Up My Heart And
                                                    Mind To:

Today's Blood Pressure: _____   Today's Sugar Count: _____

180   Continue To The Next Page

THE WEALTH IN MY HEALTH

For Breakfast Today I Had:

For Lunch Today I Had:

For Dinner Today I Had:

Today I Snacked On:

Today's Water Intake:

Today's Supplements Were:

Today's Exercise/Physical Activity Was (State What It Was And For How Long):

Today's Compliment To Myself:

Today I Imagined Myself:

Although I Wanted To

_____, I

_____

_____.

A Characteristic That I Am Choosing To Improve On:

I DIDN'T COME THIS FAR TO ONLY COME THIS FAR.

WHOLENESS NOTES

THE WEALTH IN MY HEALTH

MORNING ACTIONS AND THOUGHTS

Today:

Mood:

Today's Physical Goal:

Today I Need:

Today I Am Showing Appreciation To My Body By:

I Will Give Myself What I Need Today By:

Today I Am Choosing To Believe:

I Know I Do Not Need:

Today I Am Replacing An Old Belief With This New Belief (State The New Belief):

Today's Physical Activity Is:

I Will Support My New Beliefs By:

Today I Am Opening Up My Heart And Mind To:

Today's Blood Pressure: _____ Today's Sugar Count: _____

184

Continue To The Next Page

THE WEALTH IN MY HEALTH

For Breakfast Today I Had:

Today's Exercise/Physical Activity Was (State What It Was And For How Long):

For Lunch Today I Had:

Today's Compliment To Myself:

For Dinner Today I Had:

Today I Imagined Myself:

Today I Snacked On:

Although I Wanted To

_____, I

Today's Water Intake:

_____

_____.

Today's Supplements Were:

A Characteristic That I Am Choosing To Improve On:

THE WEALTH IN MY HEALTH

MORNING ACTIONS AND THOUGHTS

Today: Mood:

Today's Physical Goal: Today I Need:

Today I Am Showing Appreciation To My   I Will Give Myself What I Need Today By:
Body By:

Today I Am Choosing To Believe: I Know I Do Not Need:

Today I Am Replacing An Old Belief With   Today's Physical Activity Is:
This New Belief (State The New Belief):

I Will Support My New Beliefs By: Today I Am Opening Up My Heart And
                                                Mind To:

Today's Blood Pressure: _____ Today's Sugar Count: _____

186   Continue To The Next Page

THE WEALTH IN MY HEALTH

For Breakfast Today I Had:

Today's Exercise/Physical Activity Was (State What It Was And For How Long):

For Lunch Today I Had:

Today's Compliment To Myself:

For Dinner Today I Had:

Today I Imagined Myself:

Today I Snacked On:

Although I Wanted To

_____, I

Today's Water Intake:

_____

_____.

Today's Supplements Were:

A Characteristic That I Am Choosing To Improve On:

THE WEALTH IN MY HEALTH

Today:

Today's Physical Goal:

Today I Am Showing Appreciation To My Body By:

Today I Am Choosing To Believe:

Today I Am Replacing An Old Belief With This New Belief (State The New Belief):

I Will Support My New Beliefs By:

Mood:

Today I Need:

I Will Give Myself What I Need Today By:

I Know I Do Not Need:

Today's Physical Activity Is:

Today I Am Opening Up My Heart And Mind To:

Today's Blood Pressure: _____ Today's Sugar Count: _____

188   Continue To The Next Page

THE WEALTH IN MY HEALTH

For Breakfast Today I Had:

Today's Exercise/Physical Activity Was (State What It Was And For How Long):

For Lunch Today I Had:

Today's Compliment To Myself:

For Dinner Today I Had:

Today I Imagined Myself:

Today I Snacked On:

Although I Wanted To

_____, I

Today's Water Intake:

_____

_____.

Today's Supplements Were:

A Characteristic That I Am Choosing To Improve On:

WHOLENESS NOTES

NO MISTAKE WILL PREVENT ME FROM ETHICALLY AND MORALLY IMPROVING MY WELLBEING.

THE WEALTH IN MY HEALTH

MORNING ACTIONS AND THOUGHTS

Today: | Mood:

Today's Physical Goal: | Today I Need:

Today I Am Showing Appreciation To My Body By: | I Will Give Myself What I Need Today By:

Today I Am Choosing To Believe: | I Know I Do Not Need:

Today I Am Replacing An Old Belief With This New Belief (State The New Belief): | Today's Physical Activity Is:

I Will Support My New Beliefs By: | Today I Am Opening Up My Heart And Mind To:

Today's Blood Pressure: _____ Today's Sugar Count: _____

192

THE WEALTH IN MY HEALTH

For Breakfast Today I Had:

Today's Exercise/Physical Activity Was
(State What It Was And For How Long):

For Lunch Today I Had:

Today's Compliment To Myself:

For Dinner Today I Had:

Today I Imagined Myself:

Today I Snacked On:

Although I Wanted To

_____, I

Today's Water Intake:

_____

_____.

Today's Supplements Were:

A Characteristic That I Am Choosing To
Improve On:

THE WEALTH IN MY HEALTH
MORNING ACTIONS AND THOUGHTS

Today: Mood:

Today's Physical Goal: Today I Need:

Today I Am Showing Appreciation To My   I Will Give Myself What I Need Today By:
Body By:

Today I Am Choosing To Believe: I Know I Do Not Need:

Today I Am Replacing An Old Belief With   Today's Physical Activity Is:
This New Belief (State The New Belief):

I Will Support My New Beliefs By: Today I Am Opening Up My Heart And
                                                Mind To:

Today's Blood Pressure: _____ Today's Sugar Count: _____

194   Continue To The Next Page

THE WEALTH IN MY HEALTH

For Breakfast Today I Had:

Today's Exercise/Physical Activity Was
(State What It Was And For How Long):

For Lunch Today I Had:

Today's Compliment To Myself:

For Dinner Today I Had:

Today I Imagined Myself:

Today I Snacked On:

Although I Wanted To

_____, I

Today's Water Intake:

_____

_____.

Today's Supplements Were:

A Characteristic That I Am Choosing To
Improve On:

A MOMENT THAT DRASTICALLY CHANGED MY LIFE (FOR THE BETTER)

THE WEALTH IN MY HEALTH

Today: Mood:

Today's Physical Goal: Today I Need:

Today I Am Showing Appreciation To My   I Will Give Myself What I Need Today By:
Body By:

Today I Am Choosing To Believe: I Know I Do Not Need:

Today I Am Replacing An Old Belief With   Today's Physical Activity Is:
This New Belief (State The New Belief):

I Will Support My New Beliefs By: Today I Am Opening Up My Heart And
                                                Mind To:

Today's Blood Pressure: _____ Today's Sugar Count: _____

Continue To The Next Page   **197**

For Breakfast Today I Had:

Today's Exercise/Physical Activity Was
(State What It Was And For How Long):

For Lunch Today I Had:

Today's Compliment To Myself:

For Dinner Today I Had:

Today I Imagined Myself:

Today I Snacked On:

Although I Wanted To

_____, I

Today's Water Intake:

_____

_____.

Today's Supplements Were:

A Characteristic That I Am Choosing To
Improve On:

Affirmation #57: My Heart Is Strong And Healthy.

THE WEALTH IN MY HEALTH

MORNING ACTIONS AND THOUGHTS

Today: Mood:

Today's Physical Goal: Today I Need:

Today I Am Showing Appreciation To My   I Will Give Myself What I Need Today By:
Body By:

Today I Am Choosing To Believe: I Know I Do Not Need:

Today I Am Replacing An Old Belief With   Today's Physical Activity Is:
This New Belief (State The New Belief):

I Will Support My New Beliefs By: Today I Am Opening Up My Heart And
                                          Mind To:

Today's Blood Pressure: _____ Today's Sugar Count: _____

Continue To The Next Page   **199**

THE WEALTH IN MY HEALTH

For Breakfast Today I Had:

Today's Exercise/Physical Activity Was (State What It Was And For How Long):

For Lunch Today I Had:

Today's Compliment To Myself:

For Dinner Today I Had:

Today I Imagined Myself:

Today I Snacked On:

Although I Wanted To

_____, I

Today's Water Intake:

_____

_____.

Today's Supplements Were:

A Characteristic That I Am Choosing To Improve On:

THE WEALTH IN MY HEALTH

Today:

Mood:

Today's Physical Goal:

Today I Need:

Today I Am Showing Appreciation To My Body By:

I Will Give Myself What I Need Today By:

Today I Am Choosing To Believe:

I Know I Do Not Need:

Today I Am Replacing An Old Belief With This New Belief (State The New Belief):

Today's Physical Activity Is:

I Will Support My New Beliefs By:

Today I Am Opening Up My Heart And Mind To:

Today's Blood Pressure: _____ Today's Sugar Count: _____

THE WEALTH IN MY HEALTH

For Breakfast Today I Had:

Today's Exercise/Physical Activity Was
(State What It Was And For How Long):

For Lunch Today I Had:

Today's Compliment To Myself:

For Dinner Today I Had:

Today I Imagined Myself:

Today I Snacked On:

Although I Wanted To

_____, I

Today's Water Intake:

_____

_____.

Today's Supplements Were:

A Characteristic That I Am Choosing To
Improve On:

Affirmation #59: I Naturally Think Positive About Myself.

ANYTIME I EXPERIENCE DEPRESSION I

THE WEALTH IN MY HEALTH

MORNING ACTIONS AND THOUGHTS

Today: Mood:

Today's Physical Goal: Today I Need:

Today I Am Showing Appreciation To My   I Will Give Myself What I Need Today By:
Body By:

Today I Am Choosing To Believe: I Know I Do Not Need:

Today I Am Replacing An Old Belief With   Today's Physical Activity Is:
This New Belief (State The New Belief):

I Will Support My New Beliefs By: Today I Am Opening Up My Heart And
                                                Mind To:

Today's Blood Pressure: _____ Today's Sugar Count: _____

Continue To The Next Page

THE WEALTH IN MY HEALTH

For Breakfast Today I Had:

Today's Exercise/Physical Activity Was
(State What It Was And For How Long):

For Lunch Today I Had:

Today's Compliment To Myself:

For Dinner Today I Had:

Today I Imagined Myself:

Today I Snacked On:

Although I Wanted To

_____, I

Today's Water Intake:

_____

_____.

Today's Supplements Were:

A Characteristic That I Am Choosing To
Improve On:

THE WEALTH IN MY HEALTH

Today:

Mood:

Today's Physical Goal:

Today I Need:

Today I Am Showing Appreciation To My Body By:

I Will Give Myself What I Need Today By:

Today I Am Choosing To Believe:

I Know I Do Not Need:

Today I Am Replacing An Old Belief With This New Belief (State The New Belief):

Today's Physical Activity Is:

I Will Support My New Beliefs By:

Today I Am Opening Up My Heart And Mind To:

Today's Blood Pressure: _____ Today's Sugar Count: _____

Continue To The Next Page

THE WEALTH IN MY HEALTH
NIGHT ACTIONS AND THOUGHTS

For Breakfast Today I Had:

Today's Exercise/Physical Activity Was (State What It Was And For How Long):

For Lunch Today I Had:

Today's Compliment To Myself:

For Dinner Today I Had:

Today I Imagined Myself:

Today I Snacked On:

Although I Wanted To

_____, I

Today's Water Intake:

_____

_____.

Today's Supplements Were:

A Characteristic That I Am Choosing To Improve On:

I COMBAT DEPRESSION BY

WHOLENESS NOTES

THE WEALTH IN MY HEALTH

MORNING ACTIONS AND THOUGHTS

Today: Mood:

Today's Physical Goal: Today I Need:

Today I Am Showing Appreciation To My   I Will Give Myself What I Need Today By:
Body By:

Today I Am Choosing To Believe: I Know I Do Not Need:

Today I Am Replacing An Old Belief With   Today's Physical Activity Is:
This New Belief (State The New Belief):

I Will Support My New Beliefs By: Today I Am Opening Up My Heart And
                                          Mind To:

Today's Blood Pressure: _____ Today's Sugar Count: _____

210   Continue To The Next Page

THE WEALTH IN MY HEALTH

For Breakfast Today I Had:

Today's Exercise/Physical Activity Was (State What It Was And For How Long):

For Lunch Today I Had:

Today's Compliment To Myself:

For Dinner Today I Had:

Today I Imagined Myself:

Today I Snacked On:

Although I Wanted To

_____, I

Today's Water Intake:

_____

_____.

Today's Supplements Were:

A Characteristic That I Am Choosing To Improve On:

THE WEALTH IN MY HEALTH

MORNING ACTIONS AND THOUGHTS

Today: | Mood:

Today's Physical Goal: | Today I Need:

Today I Am Showing Appreciation To My Body By: | I Will Give Myself What I Need Today By:

Today I Am Choosing To Believe: | I Know I Do Not Need:

Today I Am Replacing An Old Belief With This New Belief (State The New Belief): | Today's Physical Activity Is:

I Will Support My New Beliefs By: | Today I Am Opening Up My Heart And Mind To:

Today's Blood Pressure: _____ Today's Sugar Count: _____

212 Continue To The Next Page

THE WEALTH IN MY HEALTH

NIGHT ACTIONS AND THOUGHTS

For Breakfast Today I Had:

For Lunch Today I Had:

For Dinner Today I Had:

Today I Snacked On:

Today's Water Intake:

Today's Supplements Were:

Today's Exercise/Physical Activity Was (State What It Was And For How Long):

Today's Compliment To Myself:

Today I Imagined Myself:

Although I Wanted To

_____, I

_____

_____.

A Characteristic That I Am Choosing To Improve On:

NO LONGER WILL I ALLOW OTHER PEOPLE'S FEELINGS TO DETERMINE MY SELF WORTH.

THE WEALTH IN MY HEALTH

Today: Mood:

Today's Physical Goal: Today I Need:

Today I Am Showing Appreciation To My   I Will Give Myself What I Need Today By:
Body By:

Today I Am Choosing To Believe: I Know I Do Not Need:

Today I Am Replacing An Old Belief With   Today's Physical Activity Is:
This New Belief (State The New Belief):

I Will Support My New Beliefs By: Today I Am Opening Up My Heart And
                                          Mind To:

Today's Blood Pressure: _____ Today's Sugar Count: _____

Continue To The Next Page

THE WEALTH IN MY HEALTH

NIGHT ACTIONS AND THOUGHTS

For Breakfast Today I Had:

Today's Exercise/Physical Activity Was
(State What It Was And For How Long):

For Lunch Today I Had:

Today's Compliment To Myself:

For Dinner Today I Had:

Today I Imagined Myself:

Today I Snacked On:

Although I Wanted To

_____, I

Today's Water Intake:

_____

_____.

Today's Supplements Were:

A Characteristic That I Am Choosing To
Improve On:

*Affirmation #64: I Am Grateful For My Healthy
And Beautiful Body.*

THE WEALTH IN MY HEALTH

MORNING ACTIONS AND THOUGHTS

Today: Mood:

Today's Physical Goal: Today I Need:

Today I Am Showing Appreciation To My   I Will Give Myself What I Need Today By:
Body By:

Today I Am Choosing To Believe: I Know I Do Not Need:

Today I Am Replacing An Old Belief With   Today's Physical Activity Is:
This New Belief (State The New Belief):

I Will Support My New Beliefs By: Today I Am Opening Up My Heart And
                                          Mind To:

Today's Blood Pressure: _____ Today's Sugar Count: _____

Continue To The Next Page

THE WEALTH IN MY HEALTH

For Breakfast Today I Had:

Today's Exercise/Physical Activity Was (State What It Was And For How Long):

For Lunch Today I Had:

Today's Compliment To Myself:

For Dinner Today I Had:

Today I Imagined Myself:

Today I Snacked On:

Although I Wanted To

_____, I

Today's Water Intake:

_____

_____.

Today's Supplements Were:

A Characteristic That I Am Choosing To Improve On:

Affirmation #65: Every Part Of My Body Works Well Together And Easily Manages Its Assigned Tasks.

THE WEALTH IN MY HEALTH

MORNING ACTIONS AND THOUGHTS

Today:

Mood:

Today's Physical Goal:

Today I Need:

Today I Am Showing Appreciation To My Body By:

I Will Give Myself What I Need Today By:

Today I Am Choosing To Believe:

I Know I Do Not Need:

Today I Am Replacing An Old Belief With This New Belief (State The New Belief):

Today's Physical Activity Is:

I Will Support My New Beliefs By:

Today I Am Opening Up My Heart And Mind To:

Today's Blood Pressure: _____ Today's Sugar Count: _____

Continue To The Next Page

THE WEALTH IN MY HEALTH

NIGHT ACTIONS AND THOUGHTS

For Breakfast Today I Had:

For Lunch Today I Had:

For Dinner Today I Had:

Today I Snacked On:

Today's Water Intake:

Today's Supplements Were:

Today's Exercise/Physical Activity Was (State What It Was And For How Long):

Today's Compliment To Myself:

Today I Imagined Myself:

Although I Wanted To

_____, I

_____

_____.

A Characteristic That I Am Choosing To Improve On:

Affirmation #66: I Am Always Well. I Am Always Well. I Am Always Well.

MY QUALITY
OF LIFE
HAS
IMPROVED
BECAUSE
MY
THOUGHTS
HAVE
IMPROVED.
NOW I AM
LIVING.

THE WEALTH IN MY HEALTH

MORNING ACTIONS AND THOUGHTS

Today:

Mood:

Today's Physical Goal:

Today I Need:

Today I Am Showing Appreciation To My Body By:

I Will Give Myself What I Need Today By:

Today I Am Choosing To Believe:

I Know I Do Not Need:

Today I Am Replacing An Old Belief With This New Belief (State The New Belief):

Today's Physical Activity Is:

I Will Support My New Beliefs By:

Today I Am Opening Up My Heart And Mind To:

Today's Blood Pressure: _____ Today's Sugar Count: _____

222

Continue To The Next Page

THE WEALTH IN MY HEALTH

For Breakfast Today I Had:

Today's Exercise/Physical Activity Was (State What It Was And For How Long):

For Lunch Today I Had:

Today's Compliment To Myself:

For Dinner Today I Had:

Today I Imagined Myself:

Today I Snacked On:

Although I Wanted To

_____, I

Today's Water Intake:

_____

_____.

Today's Supplements Were:

A Characteristic That I Am Choosing To Improve On:

THE WEALTH IN MY HEALTH

Today: Mood:

Today's Physical Goal: Today I Need:

Today I Am Showing Appreciation To My   I Will Give Myself What I Need Today By:
Body By:

Today I Am Choosing To Believe: I Know I Do Not Need:

Today I Am Replacing An Old Belief With   Today's Physical Activity Is:
This New Belief (State The New Belief):

I Will Support My New Beliefs By: Today I Am Opening Up My Heart And
                                          Mind To:

Today's Blood Pressure: _____ Today's Sugar Count: _____

224   Continue To The Next Page

THE WEALTH IN MY HEALTH

For Breakfast Today I Had:

For Lunch Today I Had:

For Dinner Today I Had:

Today I Snacked On:

Today's Water Intake:

Today's Supplements Were:

Today's Exercise/Physical Activity Was (State What It Was And For How Long):

Today's Compliment To Myself:

Today I Imagined Myself:

Although I Wanted To

_____, I

_____

_____.

A Characteristic That I Am Choosing To Improve On:

EVERY PHYSICAL, MENTAL AND EMOTIONAL GOAL I HAVE FOR MYSELF, I WILL OBTAIN.

EVEN WHEN IT IS EASY TO DO WHAT FEELS RIGHT, I AM TRAINING MY MIND, BODY AND SPIRIT TO DO WHAT IS BEST.

THE WEALTH IN MY HEALTH

MORNING ACTIONS AND THOUGHTS

Today: Mood:

Today's Physical Goal: Today I Need:

Today I Am Showing Appreciation To My   I Will Give Myself What I Need Today By:
Body By:

Today I Am Choosing To Believe: I Know I Do Not Need:

Today I Am Replacing An Old Belief With   Today's Physical Activity Is:
This New Belief (State The New Belief):

I Will Support My New Beliefs By: Today I Am Opening Up My Heart And
                                                Mind To:

Today's Blood Pressure: _____   Today's Sugar Count: _____

Continue To The Next Page

THE WEALTH IN MY HEALTH

For Breakfast Today I Had:

Today's Exercise/Physical Activity Was
(State What It Was And For How Long):

For Lunch Today I Had:

Today's Compliment To Myself:

For Dinner Today I Had:

Today I Imagined Myself:

Today I Snacked On:

Although I Wanted To

_____, I

Today's Water Intake:

_____

_____.

Today's Supplements Were:

A Characteristic That I Am Choosing To
Improve On:

THE WEALTH IN MY HEALTH

Today:

Mood:

Today's Physical Goal:

Today I Need:

Today I Am Showing Appreciation To My Body By:

I Will Give Myself What I Need Today By:

Today I Am Choosing To Believe:

I Know I Do Not Need:

Today I Am Replacing An Old Belief With This New Belief (State The New Belief):

Today's Physical Activity Is:

I Will Support My New Beliefs By:

Today I Am Opening Up My Heart And Mind To:

Today's Blood Pressure: _____ Today's Sugar Count: _____

Continue To The Next Page

THE WEALTH IN MY HEALTH

For Breakfast Today I Had:

Today's Exercise/Physical Activity Was (State What It Was And For How Long):

For Lunch Today I Had:

Today's Compliment To Myself:

For Dinner Today I Had:

Today I Imagined Myself:

Today I Snacked On:

Although I Wanted To

_____, I

Today's Water Intake:

_____

_____.

Today's Supplements Were:

A Characteristic That I Am Choosing To Improve On:

THE WEALTH IN MY HEALTH

MORNING ACTIONS AND THOUGHTS

Today: Mood:

Today's Physical Goal: Today I Need:

Today I Am Showing Appreciation To My   I Will Give Myself What I Need Today By:
Body By:

Today I Am Choosing To Believe: I Know I Do Not Need:

Today I Am Replacing An Old Belief With   Today's Physical Activity Is:
This New Belief (State The New Belief):

I Will Support My New Beliefs By: Today I Am Opening Up My Heart And
                                                   Mind To:

Today's Blood Pressure: _____ Today's Sugar Count: _____

232   Continue To The Next Page

THE WEALTH IN MY HEALTH

For Breakfast Today I Had:

Today's Exercise/Physical Activity Was (State What It Was And For How Long):

For Lunch Today I Had:

Today's Compliment To Myself:

For Dinner Today I Had:

Today I Imagined Myself:

Today I Snacked On:

Although I Wanted To

_____, I

Today's Water Intake:

_____

_____.

Today's Supplements Were:

A Characteristic That I Am Choosing To Improve On:

I STILL HAVE A HEART OF GOLD.

THE WEALTH IN MY HEALTH

MORNING ACTIONS AND THOUGHTS

Today:

Mood:

Today's Physical Goal:

Today I Need:

Today I Am Showing Appreciation To My Body By:

I Will Give Myself What I Need Today By:

Today I Am Choosing To Believe:

I Know I Do Not Need:

Today I Am Replacing An Old Belief With This New Belief (State The New Belief):

Today's Physical Activity Is:

I Will Support My New Beliefs By:

Today I Am Opening Up My Heart And Mind To:

Today's Blood Pressure: _____ Today's Sugar Count: _____

Continue To The Next Page

THE WEALTH IN MY HEALTH

NIGHT ACTIONS AND THOUGHTS

For Breakfast Today I Had:

For Lunch Today I Had:

For Dinner Today I Had:

Today I Snacked On:

Today's Water Intake:

Today's Supplements Were:

Today's Exercise/Physical Activity Was (State What It Was And For How Long):

Today's Compliment To Myself:

Today I Imagined Myself:

Although I Wanted To

_____, I

_____

_____.

A Characteristic That I Am Choosing To Improve On:

Affirmation #72: I Will Always Persist With Confidence.

THE WEALTH IN MY HEALTH

MORNING ACTIONS AND THOUGHTS

Today: Mood:

Today's Physical Goal: Today I Need:

Today I Am Showing Appreciation To My   I Will Give Myself What I Need Today By:
Body By:

Today I Am Choosing To Believe: I Know I Do Not Need:

Today I Am Replacing An Old Belief With   Today's Physical Activity Is:
This New Belief (State The New Belief):

I Will Support My New Beliefs By: Today I Am Opening Up My Heart And
                                          Mind To:

Today's Blood Pressure: _____ Today's Sugar Count: _____

Continue To The Next Page

237

THE WEALTH IN MY HEALTH

For Breakfast Today I Had:

Today's Exercise/Physical Activity Was (State What It Was And For How Long):

For Lunch Today I Had:

Today's Compliment To Myself:

For Dinner Today I Had:

Today I Imagined Myself:

Today I Snacked On:

Although I Wanted To

_____, I

Today's Water Intake:

_____

_____.

Today's Supplements Were:

A Characteristic That I Am Choosing To Improve On:

Affirmation #73: It Is Easy For Me To Wake Up Happy And Motivated.

THE WEALTH IN MY HEALTH

MORNING ACTIONS AND THOUGHTS

Today: Mood:

Today's Physical Goal: Today I Need:

Today I Am Showing Appreciation To My   I Will Give Myself What I Need Today By:
Body By:

Today I Am Choosing To Believe: I Know I Do Not Need:

Today I Am Replacing An Old Belief With   Today's Physical Activity Is:
This New Belief (State The New Belief):

I Will Support My New Beliefs By: Today I Am Opening Up My Heart And
                                                Mind To:

Today's Blood Pressure: _____ Today's Sugar Count: _____

Continue To The Next Page

THE WEALTH IN MY HEALTH

For Breakfast Today I Had:

Today's Exercise/Physical Activity Was (State What It Was And For How Long):

For Lunch Today I Had:

Today's Compliment To Myself:

For Dinner Today I Had:

Today I Imagined Myself:

Today I Snacked On:

Although I Wanted To

_____, I

Today's Water Intake:

_____

_____.

Today's Supplements Were:

A Characteristic That I Am Choosing To Improve On:

Affirmation #74: My Thoughts, Feelings And Actions Are Nourishing.

I GOT THROUGH BY CRYING THROUGH THE PAIN.

THE WEALTH IN MY HEALTH

Today:

Mood:

Today's Physical Goal:

Today I Need:

Today I Am Showing Appreciation To My Body By:

I Will Give Myself What I Need Today By:

Today I Am Choosing To Believe:

I Know I Do Not Need:

Today I Am Replacing An Old Belief With This New Belief (State The New Belief):

Today's Physical Activity Is:

I Will Support My New Beliefs By:

Today I Am Opening Up My Heart And Mind To:

Today's Blood Pressure: _____ Today's Sugar Count: _____

THE WEALTH IN MY HEALTH

For Breakfast Today I Had:

Today's Exercise/Physical Activity Was
(State What It Was And For How Long):

For Lunch Today I Had:

Today's Compliment To Myself:

For Dinner Today I Had:

Today I Imagined Myself:

Today I Snacked On:

Although I Wanted To

_____, I

Today's Water Intake:

_____

_____.

Today's Supplements Were:

A Characteristic That I Am Choosing To
Improve On:

THE WEALTH IN MY HEALTH

Today:

Mood:

Today's Physical Goal:

Today I Need:

Today I Am Showing Appreciation To My Body By:

I Will Give Myself What I Need Today By:

Today I Am Choosing To Believe:

I Know I Do Not Need:

Today I Am Replacing An Old Belief With This New Belief (State The New Belief):

Today's Physical Activity Is:

I Will Support My New Beliefs By:

Today I Am Opening Up My Heart And Mind To:

Today's Blood Pressure: _____ Today's Sugar Count: _____

244

Continue To The Next Page

THE WEALTH IN MY HEALTH

For Breakfast Today I Had:

Today's Exercise/Physical Activity Was (State What It Was And For How Long):

For Lunch Today I Had:

Today's Compliment To Myself:

For Dinner Today I Had:

Today I Imagined Myself:

Today I Snacked On:

Although I Wanted To

_____, I

Today's Water Intake:

_____

_____.

Today's Supplements Were:

A Characteristic That I Am Choosing To Improve On:

WHOLENESS NOTES

THE WEALTH IN MY HEALTH

Today: Mood:

Today's Physical Goal: Today I Need:

Today I Am Showing Appreciation To My   I Will Give Myself What I Need Today By:
Body By:

Today I Am Choosing To Believe: I Know I Do Not Need:

Today I Am Replacing An Old Belief With   Today's Physical Activity Is:
This New Belief (State The New Belief):

I Will Support My New Beliefs By: Today I Am Opening Up My Heart And
                                                Mind To:

Today's Blood Pressure: _____ Today's Sugar Count: _____

Continue To The Next Page

THE WEALTH IN MY HEALTH

NIGHT ACTIONS AND THOUGHTS

For Breakfast Today I Had:

Today's Exercise/Physical Activity Was
(State What It Was And For How Long):

For Lunch Today I Had:

Today's Compliment To Myself:

For Dinner Today I Had:

Today I Imagined Myself:

Today I Snacked On:

Although I Wanted To

_____, I

Today's Water Intake:

_____

_____.

Today's Supplements Were:

A Characteristic That I Am Choosing To
Improve On:

Affirmation #77: I Am Amazing Just As I Am.

THE WEALTH IN MY HEALTH

MORNING ACTIONS AND THOUGHTS

Today: Mood:

Today's Physical Goal: Today I Need:

Today I Am Showing Appreciation To My   I Will Give Myself What I Need Today By:
Body By:

Today I Am Choosing To Believe: I Know I Do Not Need:

Today I Am Replacing An Old Belief With   Today's Physical Activity Is:
This New Belief (State The New Belief):

I Will Support My New Beliefs By: Today I Am Opening Up My Heart And
                                                Mind To:

Today's Blood Pressure: _____ Today's Sugar Count: _____

Continue To The Next Page   **249**

THE WEALTH IN MY HEALTH

For Breakfast Today I Had:

Today's Exercise/Physical Activity Was (State What It Was And For How Long):

For Lunch Today I Had:

Today's Compliment To Myself:

For Dinner Today I Had:

Today I Imagined Myself:

Today I Snacked On:

Although I Wanted To

_____, I

Today's Water Intake:

_____

_____.

Today's Supplements Were:

A Characteristic That I Am Choosing To Improve On:

Affirmation #78: Obstacles Give Me Strength. I Quickly Respond To Obstacles With Healthy And Positive Solutions.

TEN PERSONAL FAVORITE DAILY HEALTH AFFIRMATIONS

THE WEALTH IN MY HEALTH

MORNING ACTIONS AND THOUGHTS

Today: Mood:

Today's Physical Goal: Today I Need:

Today I Am Showing Appreciation To My   I Will Give Myself What I Need Today By:
Body By:

Today I Am Choosing To Believe: I Know I Do Not Need:

Today I Am Replacing An Old Belief With   Today's Physical Activity Is:
This New Belief (State The New Belief):

I Will Support My New Beliefs By: Today I Am Opening Up My Heart And
                                                    Mind To:

Today's Blood Pressure: _____ Today's Sugar Count: _____

252   Continue To The Next Page

THE WEALTH IN MY HEALTH
NIGHT ACTIONS AND THOUGHTS

For Breakfast Today I Had:

For Lunch Today I Had:

For Dinner Today I Had:

Today I Snacked On:

Today's Water Intake:

Today's Supplements Were:

Today's Exercise/Physical Activity Was (State What It Was And For How Long):

Today's Compliment To Myself:

Today I Imagined Myself:

Although I Wanted To

_____, I

_____

_____.

A Characteristic That I Am Choosing To Improve On:

THE WEALTH IN MY HEALTH

Today: Mood:

Today's Physical Goal: Today I Need:

Today I Am Showing Appreciation To My   I Will Give Myself What I Need Today By:
Body By:

Today I Am Choosing To Believe: I Know I Do Not Need:

Today I Am Replacing An Old Belief With   Today's Physical Activity Is:
This New Belief (State The New Belief):

I Will Support My New Beliefs By: Today I Am Opening Up My Heart And
                                                    Mind To:

Today's Blood Pressure: _____ Today's Sugar Count: _____

254   Continue To The Next Page

THE WEALTH IN MY HEALTH

For Breakfast Today I Had:

For Lunch Today I Had:

For Dinner Today I Had:

Today I Snacked On:

Today's Water Intake:

Today's Supplements Were:

Today's Exercise/Physical Activity Was (State What It Was And For How Long):

Today's Compliment To Myself:

Today I Imagined Myself:

Although I Wanted To

_____, I

_____

_____.

A Characteristic That I Am Choosing To Improve On:

THE WEALTH IN MY HEALTH

MORNING ACTIONS AND THOUGHTS

Today: Mood:

Today's Physical Goal: Today I Need:

Today I Am Showing Appreciation To My   I Will Give Myself What I Need Today By:
Body By:

Today I Am Choosing To Believe: I Know I Do Not Need:

Today I Am Replacing An Old Belief With   Today's Physical Activity Is:
This New Belief (State The New Belief):

I Will Support My New Beliefs By: Today I Am Opening Up My Heart And
                                                Mind To:

Today's Blood Pressure: _____ Today's Sugar Count: _____

Continue To The Next Page

THE WEALTH IN MY HEALTH

For Breakfast Today I Had:

Today's Exercise/Physical Activity Was (State What It Was And For How Long):

For Lunch Today I Had:

Today's Compliment To Myself:

For Dinner Today I Had:

Today I Imagined Myself:

Today I Snacked On:

Although I Wanted To

_____, I

Today's Water Intake:

_____

_____.

Today's Supplements Were:

A Characteristic That I Am Choosing To Improve On:

THE WEALTH IN MY HEALTH

Today: Mood:

Today's Physical Goal: Today I Need:

Today I Am Showing Appreciation To My   I Will Give Myself What I Need Today By:
Body By:

Today I Am Choosing To Believe: I Know I Do Not Need:

Today I Am Replacing An Old Belief With   Today's Physical Activity Is:
This New Belief (State The New Belief):

I Will Support My New Beliefs By: Today I Am Opening Up My Heart And
                                                Mind To:

Today's Blood Pressure: _____ Today's Sugar Count: _____

THE WEALTH IN MY HEALTH

For Breakfast Today I Had:

Today's Exercise/Physical Activity Was (State What It Was And For How Long):

For Lunch Today I Had:

Today's Compliment To Myself:

For Dinner Today I Had:

Today I Imagined Myself:

Today I Snacked On:

Although I Wanted To

_____, I

Today's Water Intake:

_____

_____.

Today's Supplements Were:

A Characteristic That I Am Choosing To Improve On:

I DIDN'T JUST GET BETTER AT ASKING. I ALSO GOT BETTER AT DOING.

EVERY LITTLE POSITIVE CHANGE I MAKE IS PROGRESS.

THE WEALTH IN MY HEALTH

MORNING ACTIONS AND THOUGHTS

Today:

Mood:

Today's Physical Goal:

Today I Need:

Today I Am Showing Appreciation To My Body By:

I Will Give Myself What I Need Today By:

Today I Am Choosing To Believe:

I Know I Do Not Need:

Today I Am Replacing An Old Belief With This New Belief (State The New Belief):

Today's Physical Activity Is:

I Will Support My New Beliefs By:

Today I Am Opening Up My Heart And Mind To:

Today's Blood Pressure: _____ Today's Sugar Count: _____

Continue To The Next Page

THE WEALTH IN MY HEALTH

For Breakfast Today I Had:

Today's Exercise/Physical Activity Was (State What It Was And For How Long):

For Lunch Today I Had:

Today's Compliment To Myself:

For Dinner Today I Had:

Today I Imagined Myself:

Today I Snacked On:

Although I Wanted To

_____, I

Today's Water Intake:

_____

_____.

Today's Supplements Were:

A Characteristic That I Am Choosing To Improve On:

THE WEALTH IN MY HEALTH

Today: Mood:

Today's Physical Goal: Today I Need:

Today I Am Showing Appreciation To My   I Will Give Myself What I Need Today By:
Body By:

Today I Am Choosing To Believe: I Know I Do Not Need:

Today I Am Replacing An Old Belief With   Today's Physical Activity Is:
This New Belief (State The New Belief):

I Will Support My New Beliefs By: Today I Am Opening Up My Heart And
                                          Mind To:

Today's Blood Pressure: _____ Today's Sugar Count: _____

264   Continue To The Next Page

THE WEALTH IN MY HEALTH

For Breakfast Today I Had:

Today's Exercise/Physical Activity Was (State What It Was And For How Long):

For Lunch Today I Had:

Today's Compliment To Myself:

For Dinner Today I Had:

Today I Imagined Myself:

Today I Snacked On:

Although I Wanted To

_____, I

Today's Water Intake:

_____

_____.

Today's Supplements Were:

A Characteristic That I Am Choosing To Improve On:

THE WEALTH IN MY HEALTH

MORNING ACTIONS AND THOUGHTS

Today:

Mood:

Today's Physical Goal:

Today I Need:

Today I Am Showing Appreciation To My Body By:

I Will Give Myself What I Need Today By:

Today I Am Choosing To Believe:

I Know I Do Not Need:

Today I Am Replacing An Old Belief With This New Belief (State The New Belief):

Today's Physical Activity Is:

I Will Support My New Beliefs By:

Today I Am Opening Up My Heart And Mind To:

Today's Blood Pressure: _____ Today's Sugar Count: _____

266

Continue To The Next Page

THE WEALTH IN MY HEALTH

For Breakfast Today I Had:

Today's Exercise/Physical Activity Was
(State What It Was And For How Long):

For Lunch Today I Had:

Today's Compliment To Myself:

For Dinner Today I Had:

Today I Imagined Myself:

Today I Snacked On:

Although I Wanted To

_____, I

Today's Water Intake:

_____

_____.

Today's Supplements Were:

A Characteristic That I Am Choosing To
Improve On:

THE WEALTH IN MY HEALTH

Today: Mood:

Today's Physical Goal: Today I Need:

Today I Am Showing Appreciation To My   I Will Give Myself What I Need Today By:
Body By:

Today I Am Choosing To Believe: I Know I Do Not Need:

Today I Am Replacing An Old Belief With   Today's Physical Activity Is:
This New Belief (State The New Belief):

I Will Support My New Beliefs By: Today I Am Opening Up My Heart And
                                                Mind To:

Today's Blood Pressure: _____ Today's Sugar Count: _____

268   Continue To The Next Page

THE WEALTH IN MY HEALTH

NIGHT ACTIONS AND THOUGHTS

For Breakfast Today I Had:

Today's Exercise/Physical Activity Was (State What It Was And For How Long):

For Lunch Today I Had:

Today's Compliment To Myself:

For Dinner Today I Had:

Today I Imagined Myself:

Today I Snacked On:

Although I Wanted To

_____, I

Today's Water Intake:

_____

_____.

Today's Supplements Were:

A Characteristic That I Am Choosing To Improve On:

I HAVE LEARNED TO RELAX AND NOT ALLOW PEOPLE'S WORDS TO AFFECT ME.

THE WEALTH IN MY HEALTH

Today: Mood:

Today's Physical Goal: Today I Need:

Today I Am Showing Appreciation To My   I Will Give Myself What I Need Today By:
Body By:

Today I Am Choosing To Believe: I Know I Do Not Need:

Today I Am Replacing An Old Belief With   Today's Physical Activity Is:
This New Belief (State The New Belief):

I Will Support My New Beliefs By: Today I Am Opening Up My Heart And
                                                Mind To:

Today's Blood Pressure: _____   Today's Sugar Count: _____

Continue To The Next Page   **271**

THE WEALTH IN MY HEALTH

For Breakfast Today I Had:

Today's Exercise/Physical Activity Was
(State What It Was And For How Long):

For Lunch Today I Had:

Today's Compliment To Myself:

For Dinner Today I Had:

Today I Imagined Myself:

Today I Snacked On:

Although I Wanted To

_____, I

Today's Water Intake:

_____

_____.

Today's Supplements Were:

A Characteristic That I Am Choosing To
Improve On:

Affirmation #87: Every Time I Look At Myself I See Beauty.

THE WEALTH IN MY HEALTH

Today: Mood:

Today's Physical Goal: Today I Need:

Today I Am Showing Appreciation To My   I Will Give Myself What I Need Today By:
Body By:

Today I Am Choosing To Believe: I Know I Do Not Need:

Today I Am Replacing An Old Belief With   Today's Physical Activity Is:
This New Belief (State The New Belief):

I Will Support My New Beliefs By: Today I Am Opening Up My Heart And
                                      Mind To:

Today's Blood Pressure: _____ Today's Sugar Count: _____

THE WEALTH IN MY HEALTH

For Breakfast Today I Had:

For Lunch Today I Had:

For Dinner Today I Had:

Today I Snacked On:

Today's Water Intake:

Today's Supplements Were:

Today's Exercise/Physical Activity Was (State What It Was And For How Long):

Today's Compliment To Myself:

Today I Imagined Myself:

Although I Wanted To

_____, I

_____

_____.

A Characteristic That I Am Choosing To Improve On:

Affirmation #88: It's Easy For Me To Be Healthy.

I LOVE WHO I AM BECOMING. I JUST LOVE IT.

THE WEALTH IN MY HEALTH

Today: Mood:

Today's Physical Goal: Today I Need:

Today I Am Showing Appreciation To My   I Will Give Myself What I Need Today By:
Body By:

Today I Am Choosing To Believe: I Know I Do Not Need:

Today I Am Replacing An Old Belief With   Today's Physical Activity Is:
This New Belief (State The New Belief):

I Will Support My New Beliefs By: Today I Am Opening Up My Heart And
                                                Mind To:

Today's Blood Pressure: _____ Today's Sugar Count: _____

276   Continue To The Next Page

THE WEALTH IN MY HEALTH

For Breakfast Today I Had:

Today's Exercise/Physical Activity Was (State What It Was And For How Long):

For Lunch Today I Had:

Today's Compliment To Myself:

For Dinner Today I Had:

Today I Imagined Myself:

Today I Snacked On:

Although I Wanted To

_____, I

Today's Water Intake:

_____

_____.

Today's Supplements Were:

A Characteristic That I Am Choosing To Improve On:

THE WEALTH IN MY HEALTH

Today: Mood:

Today's Physical Goal: Today I Need:

Today I Am Showing Appreciation To My   I Will Give Myself What I Need Today By:
Body By:

Today I Am Choosing To Believe: I Know I Do Not Need:

Today I Am Replacing An Old Belief With   Today's Physical Activity Is:
This New Belief (State The New Belief):

I Will Support My New Beliefs By: Today I Am Opening Up My Heart And
                                          Mind To:

Today's Blood Pressure: _____ Today's Sugar Count: _____

278   Continue To The Next Page

THE WEALTH IN MY HEALTH

For Breakfast Today I Had:

Today's Exercise/Physical Activity Was (State What It Was And For How Long):

For Lunch Today I Had:

Today's Compliment To Myself:

For Dinner Today I Had:

Today I Imagined Myself:

Today I Snacked On:

Although I Wanted To

_____, I

Today's Water Intake:

_____

_____.

Today's Supplements Were:

A Characteristic That I Am Choosing To Improve On:

THE WEALTH IN MY HEALTH

Today: Mood:

Today's Physical Goal: Today I Need:

Today I Am Showing Appreciation To My   I Will Give Myself What I Need Today By:
Body By:

Today I Am Choosing To Believe: I Know I Do Not Need:

Today I Am Replacing An Old Belief With   Today's Physical Activity Is:
This New Belief (State The New Belief):

I Will Support My New Beliefs By: Today I Am Opening Up My Heart And
                                                 Mind To:

Today's Blood Pressure: _____ Today's Sugar Count: _____

280   Continue To The Next Page

THE WEALTH IN MY HEALTH

For Breakfast Today I Had:

Today's Exercise/Physical Activity Was (State What It Was And For How Long):

For Lunch Today I Had:

Today's Compliment To Myself:

For Dinner Today I Had:

Today I Imagined Myself:

Today I Snacked On:

Although I Wanted To

_____, I

Today's Water Intake:

_____

_____.

Today's Supplements Were:

A Characteristic That I Am Choosing To Improve On:

THE WEALTH IN MY HEALTH

Today: Mood:

Today's Physical Goal: Today I Need:

Today I Am Showing Appreciation To My   I Will Give Myself What I Need Today By:
Body By:

Today I Am Choosing To Believe: I Know I Do Not Need:

Today I Am Replacing An Old Belief With   Today's Physical Activity Is:
This New Belief (State The New Belief):

I Will Support My New Beliefs By: Today I Am Opening Up My Heart And
                                                Mind To:

Today's Blood Pressure: _____ Today's Sugar Count: _____

THE WEALTH IN MY HEALTH

For Breakfast Today I Had:

Today's Exercise/Physical Activity Was
(State What It Was And For How Long):

For Lunch Today I Had:

Today's Compliment To Myself:

For Dinner Today I Had:

Today I Imagined Myself:

Today I Snacked On:

Although I Wanted To

_____, I

Today's Water Intake:

_____

_____.

Today's Supplements Were:

A Characteristic That I Am Choosing To
Improve On:

WEIGHT MATTERS
OR DOESN'T MATTER
TO ME BECAUSE

I LOVE WHAT I PUT INTO MY BODY.

THE WEALTH IN MY HEALTH

Today:

Mood:

Today's Physical Goal:

Today I Need:

Today I Am Showing Appreciation To My Body By:

I Will Give Myself What I Need Today By:

Today I Am Choosing To Believe:

I Know I Do Not Need:

Today I Am Replacing An Old Belief With This New Belief (State The New Belief):

Today's Physical Activity Is:

I Will Support My New Beliefs By:

Today I Am Opening Up My Heart And Mind To:

Today's Blood Pressure: _____ Today's Sugar Count: _____

Continue To The Next Page

THE WEALTH IN MY HEALTH

For Breakfast Today I Had:

For Lunch Today I Had:

For Dinner Today I Had:

Today I Snacked On:

Today's Water Intake:

Today's Supplements Were:

Today's Exercise/Physical Activity Was (State What It Was And For How Long):

Today's Compliment To Myself:

Today I Imagined Myself:

Although I Wanted To

_____, I

_____

_____.

A Characteristic That I Am Choosing To Improve On:

Affirmation #93: My Mind And Body Are Both Beautiful And Appealing.

287

THE WEALTH IN MY HEALTH

MORNING ACTIONS AND THOUGHTS

Today: Mood:

Today's Physical Goal: Today I Need:

Today I Am Showing Appreciation To My   I Will Give Myself What I Need Today By:
Body By:

Today I Am Choosing To Believe: I Know I Do Not Need:

Today I Am Replacing An Old Belief With   Today's Physical Activity Is:
This New Belief (State The New Belief):

I Will Support My New Beliefs By: Today I Am Opening Up My Heart And
                                          Mind To:

Today's Blood Pressure: _____ Today's Sugar Count: _____

Continue To The Next Page

THE WEALTH IN MY HEALTH

For Breakfast Today I Had:

For Lunch Today I Had:

For Dinner Today I Had:

Today I Snacked On:

Today's Water Intake:

Today's Supplements Were:

Today's Exercise/Physical Activity Was (State What It Was And For How Long):

Today's Compliment To Myself:

Today I Imagined Myself:

Although I Wanted To

_____, I

_____

_____.

A Characteristic That I Am Choosing To Improve On:

THE WEALTH IN MY HEALTH

MORNING ACTIONS AND THOUGHTS

Today: Mood:

Today's Physical Goal: Today I Need:

Today I Am Showing Appreciation To My   I Will Give Myself What I Need Today By:
Body By:

Today I Am Choosing To Believe: I Know I Do Not Need:

Today I Am Replacing An Old Belief With   Today's Physical Activity Is:
This New Belief (State The New Belief):

I Will Support My New Beliefs By: Today I Am Opening Up My Heart And
                                                Mind To:

Today's Blood Pressure: _____ Today's Sugar Count: _____

Continue To The Next Page

THE WEALTH IN MY HEALTH
NIGHT ACTIONS AND THOUGHTS

For Breakfast Today I Had:

For Lunch Today I Had:

For Dinner Today I Had:

Today I Snacked On:

Today's Water Intake:

Today's Supplements Were:

Today's Exercise/Physical Activity Was (State What It Was And For How Long):

Today's Compliment To Myself:

Today I Imagined Myself:

Although I Wanted To

_____, I

_____

_____.

A Characteristic That I Am Choosing To Improve On:

THE WEALTH IN MY HEALTH
MORNING ACTIONS AND THOUGHTS

Today: Mood:

Today's Physical Goal: Today I Need:

Today I Am Showing Appreciation To My   I Will Give Myself What I Need Today By:
Body By:

Today I Am Choosing To Believe: I Know I Do Not Need:

Today I Am Replacing An Old Belief With   Today's Physical Activity Is:
This New Belief (State The New Belief):

I Will Support My New Beliefs By: Today I Am Opening Up My Heart And
                                              Mind To:

Today's Blood Pressure: _____ Today's Sugar Count: _____

Continue To The Next Page

THE WEALTH IN MY HEALTH
NIGHT ACTIONS AND THOUGHTS

For Breakfast Today I Had:

Today's Exercise/Physical Activity Was (State What It Was And For How Long):

For Lunch Today I Had:

Today's Compliment To Myself:

For Dinner Today I Had:

Today I Imagined Myself:

Today I Snacked On:

Although I Wanted To

_____, I

Today's Water Intake:

_____

_____.

Today's Supplements Were:

A Characteristic That I Am Choosing To Improve On:

I LIKE TO USE MY IMAGINATION TO

THE WEALTH IN MY HEALTH

MORNING ACTIONS AND THOUGHTS

Today: Mood:

Today's Physical Goal: Today I Need:

Today I Am Showing Appreciation To My   I Will Give Myself What I Need Today By:
Body By:

Today I Am Choosing To Believe: I Know I Do Not Need:

Today I Am Replacing An Old Belief With   Today's Physical Activity Is:
This New Belief (State The New Belief):

I Will Support My New Beliefs By: Today I Am Opening Up My Heart And
                                                Mind To:

Today's Blood Pressure: _____ Today's Sugar Count: _____

THE WEALTH IN MY HEALTH

For Breakfast Today I Had:

Today's Exercise/Physical Activity Was (State What It Was And For How Long):

For Lunch Today I Had:

Today's Compliment To Myself:

For Dinner Today I Had:

Today I Imagined Myself:

Today I Snacked On:

Although I Wanted To

_____, I

Today's Water Intake:

_____

_____.

Today's Supplements Were:

A Characteristic That I Am Choosing To Improve On:

Affirmation #97: I Inspire Other People And I Am Highly Respected.

THE WEALTH IN MY HEALTH

MORNING ACTIONS AND THOUGHTS

Today:

Mood:

Today's Physical Goal:

Today I Need:

Today I Am Showing Appreciation To My Body By:

I Will Give Myself What I Need Today By:

Today I Am Choosing To Believe:

I Know I Do Not Need:

Today I Am Replacing An Old Belief With This New Belief (State The New Belief):

Today's Physical Activity Is:

I Will Support My New Beliefs By:

Today I Am Opening Up My Heart And Mind To:

Today's Blood Pressure: _____ Today's Sugar Count: _____

Continue To The Next Page

THE WEALTH IN MY HEALTH
NIGHT ACTIONS AND THOUGHTS

For Breakfast Today I Had:

Today's Exercise/Physical Activity Was (State What It Was And For How Long):

For Lunch Today I Had:

Today's Compliment To Myself:

For Dinner Today I Had:

Today I Imagined Myself:

Today I Snacked On:

Although I Wanted To

_____, I

Today's Water Intake:

_____

_____.

Today's Supplements Were:

A Characteristic That I Am Choosing To Improve On:

Affirmation #98: I Get Excited Every Time I Look In The Mirror.

WHOLNESS NOTES

THE WEALTH IN MY HEALTH

MORNING ACTIONS AND THOUGHTS

Today:

Mood:

Today's Physical Goal:

Today I Need:

Today I Am Showing Appreciation To My Body By:

I Will Give Myself What I Need Today By:

Today I Am Choosing To Believe:

I Know I Do Not Need:

Today I Am Replacing An Old Belief With This New Belief (State The New Belief):

Today's Physical Activity Is:

I Will Support My New Beliefs By:

Today I Am Opening Up My Heart And Mind To:

Today's Blood Pressure: _____ Today's Sugar Count: _____

300

Continue To The Next Page

THE WEALTH IN MY HEALTH

For Breakfast Today I Had:

Today's Exercise/Physical Activity Was
(State What It Was And For How Long):

For Lunch Today I Had:

Today's Compliment To Myself:

For Dinner Today I Had:

Today I Imagined Myself:

Today I Snacked On:

Although I Wanted To

_____, I

Today's Water Intake:

_____

_____.

Today's Supplements Were:

A Characteristic That I Am Choosing To
Improve On:

THE WEALTH IN MY HEALTH

Today:

Mood:

Today's Physical Goal:	Today I Need:
Today I Am Showing Appreciation To My Body By:	I Will Give Myself What I Need Today By:
Today I Am Choosing To Believe:	I Know I Do Not Need:
Today I Am Replacing An Old Belief With This New Belief (State The New Belief):	Today's Physical Activity Is:
I Will Support My New Beliefs By:	Today I Am Opening Up My Heart And Mind To:

Today's Blood Pressure: _____ Today's Sugar Count: _____

302

Continue To The Next Page

THE WEALTH IN MY HEALTH

For Breakfast Today I Had:

Today's Exercise/Physical Activity Was (State What It Was And For How Long):

For Lunch Today I Had:

Today's Compliment To Myself:

For Dinner Today I Had:

Today I Imagined Myself:

Today I Snacked On:

Although I Wanted To

_____, I

Today's Water Intake:

_____

_____.

Today's Supplements Were:

A Characteristic That I Am Choosing To Improve On:

THE WEALTH IN MY HEALTH

Today: Mood:

Today's Physical Goal: Today I Need:

Today I Am Showing Appreciation To My   I Will Give Myself What I Need Today By:
Body By:

Today I Am Choosing To Believe: I Know I Do Not Need:

Today I Am Replacing An Old Belief With   Today's Physical Activity Is:
This New Belief (State The New Belief):

I Will Support My New Beliefs By: Today I Am Opening Up My Heart And
                                          Mind To:

Today's Blood Pressure: _____ Today's Sugar Count: _____

304   Continue To The Next Page

THE WEALTH IN MY HEALTH

For Breakfast Today I Had:

Today's Exercise/Physical Activity Was (State What It Was And For How Long):

For Lunch Today I Had:

Today's Compliment To Myself:

For Dinner Today I Had:

Today I Imagined Myself:

Today I Snacked On:

Although I Wanted To

_____, I

Today's Water Intake:

_____

_____.

Today's Supplements Were:

A Characteristic That I Am Choosing To Improve On:

THE WEALTH IN MY HEALTH

MORNING ACTIONS AND THOUGHTS

Today:

Mood:

Today's Physical Goal:

Today I Need:

Today I Am Showing Appreciation To My Body By:

I Will Give Myself What I Need Today By:

Today I Am Choosing To Believe:

I Know I Do Not Need:

Today I Am Replacing An Old Belief With This New Belief (State The New Belief):

Today's Physical Activity Is:

I Will Support My New Beliefs By:

Today I Am Opening Up My Heart And Mind To:

Today's Blood Pressure: _____ Today's Sugar Count: _____

306

Continue To The Next Page

THE WEALTH IN MY HEALTH

For Breakfast Today I Had:

Today's Exercise/Physical Activity Was (State What It Was And For How Long):

For Lunch Today I Had:

Today's Compliment To Myself:

For Dinner Today I Had:

Today I Imagined Myself:

Today I Snacked On:

Although I Wanted To

_____, I

Today's Water Intake:

_____

_____.

Today's Supplements Were:

A Characteristic That I Am Choosing To Improve On:

I HAVE CHANGED. I'M NOT WHO I USED TO BE. I'M WORKING TOWARDS A BETTER ME.

THE WEALTH IN MY HEALTH

MORNING ACTIONS AND THOUGHTS

Today:

Mood:

Today's Physical Goal:

Today I Need:

Today I Am Showing Appreciation To My Body By:

I Will Give Myself What I Need Today By:

Today I Am Choosing To Believe:

I Know I Do Not Need:

Today I Am Replacing An Old Belief With This New Belief (State The New Belief):

Today's Physical Activity Is:

I Will Support My New Beliefs By:

Today I Am Opening Up My Heart And Mind To:

Today's Blood Pressure: _____ Today's Sugar Count: _____

Continue To The Next Page

THE WEALTH IN MY HEALTH

For Breakfast Today I Had:

Today's Exercise/Physical Activity Was (State What It Was And For How Long):

For Lunch Today I Had:

Today's Compliment To Myself:

For Dinner Today I Had:

Today I Imagined Myself:

Today I Snacked On:

Although I Wanted To

_____, I

Today's Water Intake:

_____

_____.

Today's Supplements Were:

A Characteristic That I Am Choosing To Improve On:

Affirmation #103: I Am Very Focused.

THE WEALTH IN MY HEALTH

Today:

Mood:

Today's Physical Goal:

Today I Need:

Today I Am Showing Appreciation To My Body By:

I Will Give Myself What I Need Today By:

Today I Am Choosing To Believe:

I Know I Do Not Need:

Today I Am Replacing An Old Belief With This New Belief (State The New Belief):

Today's Physical Activity Is:

I Will Support My New Beliefs By:

Today I Am Opening Up My Heart And Mind To:

Today's Blood Pressure: _____ Today's Sugar Count: _____

Continue To The Next Page

THE WEALTH IN MY HEALTH

NIGHT ACTIONS AND THOUGHTS

For Breakfast Today I Had:

Today's Exercise/Physical Activity Was (State What It Was And For How Long):

For Lunch Today I Had:

Today's Compliment To Myself:

For Dinner Today I Had:

Today I Imagined Myself:

Today I Snacked On:

Although I Wanted To

_____, I

Today's Water Intake:

_____

_____.

Today's Supplements Were:

A Characteristic That I Am Choosing To Improve On:

Affirmation #104: I Can Easily Express Myself In Truth With Love And Clarity.

THE WEALTH IN MY HEALTH

MORNING ACTIONS AND THOUGHTS

Today: Mood:

Today's Physical Goal: Today I Need:

Today I Am Showing Appreciation To My   I Will Give Myself What I Need Today By:
Body By:

Today I Am Choosing To Believe: I Know I Do Not Need:

Today I Am Replacing An Old Belief With   Today's Physical Activity Is:
This New Belief (State The New Belief):

I Will Support My New Beliefs By: Today I Am Opening Up My Heart And
                                                 Mind To:

Today's Blood Pressure: _____ Today's Sugar Count: _____

Continue To The Next Page

THE WEALTH IN MY HEALTH

For Breakfast Today I Had:

For Lunch Today I Had:

For Dinner Today I Had:

Today I Snacked On:

Today's Water Intake:

Today's Supplements Were:

Today's Exercise/Physical Activity Was
(State What It Was And For How Long):

Today's Compliment To Myself:

Today I Imagined Myself:

Although I Wanted To

_____, I

_____

_____.

A Characteristic That I Am Choosing To
Improve On:

THE WEALTH IN MY HEALTH

MORNING ACTIONS AND THOUGHTS

Today:

Mood:

Today's Physical Goal:

Today I Need:

Today I Am Showing Appreciation To My Body By:

I Will Give Myself What I Need Today By:

Today I Am Choosing To Believe:

I Know I Do Not Need:

Today I Am Replacing An Old Belief With This New Belief (State The New Belief):

Today's Physical Activity Is:

I Will Support My New Beliefs By:

Today I Am Opening Up My Heart And Mind To:

Today's Blood Pressure: _____ Today's Sugar Count: _____

Continue To The Next Page

THE WEALTH IN MY HEALTH

NIGHT ACTIONS AND THOUGHTS

For Breakfast Today I Had:

For Lunch Today I Had:

For Dinner Today I Had:

Today I Snacked On:

Today's Water Intake:

Today's Supplements Were:

Today's Exercise/Physical Activity Was
(State What It Was And For How Long):

Today's Compliment To Myself:

Today I Imagined Myself:

Although I Wanted To

_____, I

_____

_____.

A Characteristic That I Am Choosing To
Improve On:

Affirmation #106: I Am Filled With Self-Love And Confidence.

THE TIPS I WOULD GIVE MYSELF TO STICKING TO MY NEW & IMPROVED LIFESTYLE CHANGES ARE

THE WEALTH IN MY HEALTH

MORNING ACTIONS AND THOUGHTS

Today: Mood:

Today's Physical Goal: Today I Need:

Today I Am Showing Appreciation To My   I Will Give Myself What I Need Today By:
Body By:

Today I Am Choosing To Believe: I Know I Do Not Need:

Today I Am Replacing An Old Belief With   Today's Physical Activity Is:
This New Belief (State The New Belief):

I Will Support My New Beliefs By: Today I Am Opening Up My Heart And
                                               Mind To:

Today's Blood Pressure: _____ Today's Sugar Count: _____

THE WEALTH IN MY HEALTH

For Breakfast Today I Had:

Today's Exercise/Physical Activity Was
(State What It Was And For How Long):

For Lunch Today I Had:

Today's Compliment To Myself:

For Dinner Today I Had:

Today I Imagined Myself:

Today I Snacked On:

Although I Wanted To

_____, I

Today's Water Intake:

_____

_____.

Today's Supplements Were:

A Characteristic That I Am Choosing To
Improve On:

THE WEALTH IN MY HEALTH

MORNING ACTIONS AND THOUGHTS

Today: Mood:

Today's Physical Goal: Today I Need:

Today I Am Showing Appreciation To My   I Will Give Myself What I Need Today By:
Body By:

Today I Am Choosing To Believe: I Know I Do Not Need:

Today I Am Replacing An Old Belief With   Today's Physical Activity Is:
This New Belief (State The New Belief):

I Will Support My New Beliefs By: Today I Am Opening Up My Heart And
                                                Mind To:

Today's Blood Pressure: _____ Today's Sugar Count: _____

320   Continue To The Next Page

THE WEALTH IN MY HEALTH

For Breakfast Today I Had:

Today's Exercise/Physical Activity Was (State What It Was And For How Long):

For Lunch Today I Had:

Today's Compliment To Myself:

For Dinner Today I Had:

Today I Imagined Myself:

Today I Snacked On:

Although I Wanted To

_____, I

Today's Water Intake:

_____

_____.

Today's Supplements Were:

A Characteristic That I Am Choosing To Improve On:

WHEN I SHOP FOR FOOD, I NOW LOOK FOR

THE WEALTH IN MY HEALTH

MORNING ACTIONS AND THOUGHTS

Today:

Mood:

Today's Physical Goal:

Today I Need:

Today I Am Showing Appreciation To My Body By:

I Will Give Myself What I Need Today By:

Today I Am Choosing To Believe:

I Know I Do Not Need:

Today I Am Replacing An Old Belief With This New Belief (State The New Belief):

Today's Physical Activity Is:

I Will Support My New Beliefs By:

Today I Am Opening Up My Heart And Mind To:

Today's Blood Pressure: _____ Today's Sugar Count: _____

Continue To The Next Page

THE WEALTH IN MY HEALTH

For Breakfast Today I Had:

Today's Exercise/Physical Activity Was
(State What It Was And For How Long):

For Lunch Today I Had:

Today's Compliment To Myself:

For Dinner Today I Had:

Today I Imagined Myself:

Today I Snacked On:

Although I Wanted To

_____, I

Today's Water Intake:

_____

_____.

Today's Supplements Were:

A Characteristic That I Am Choosing To
Improve On:

Affirmation #109: I Feel Great In My Own Skin.

THE WEALTH IN MY HEALTH

MORNING ACTIONS AND THOUGHTS

Today: Mood:

Today's Physical Goal: Today I Need:

Today I Am Showing Appreciation To My   I Will Give Myself What I Need Today By:
Body By:

Today I Am Choosing To Believe: I Know I Do Not Need:

Today I Am Replacing An Old Belief With   Today's Physical Activity Is:
This New Belief (State The New Belief):

I Will Support My New Beliefs By: Today I Am Opening Up My Heart And
                                          Mind To:

Today's Blood Pressure: _____ Today's Sugar Count: _____

Continue To The Next Page

THE WEALTH IN MY HEALTH

For Breakfast Today I Had:

Today's Exercise/Physical Activity Was
(State What It Was And For How Long):

For Lunch Today I Had:

Today's Compliment To Myself:

For Dinner Today I Had:

Today I Imagined Myself:

Today I Snacked On:

Although I Wanted To

_____, I

Today's Water Intake:

_____

_____.

Today's Supplements Were:

A Characteristic That I Am Choosing To
Improve On:

Affirmation #110: I Am Turning My Wounds Into Wisdom.

THE WEALTH IN MY HEALTH

Today: Mood:

Today's Physical Goal: Today I Need:

Today I Am Showing Appreciation To My Body By: I Will Give Myself What I Need Today By:

Today I Am Choosing To Believe: I Know I Do Not Need:

Today I Am Replacing An Old Belief With This New Belief (State The New Belief):   Today's Physical Activity Is:

I Will Support My New Beliefs By: Today I Am Opening Up My Heart And Mind To:

Today's Blood Pressure: _____ Today's Sugar Count: _____

Continue To The Next Page

THE WEALTH IN MY HEALTH

NIGHT ACTIONS AND THOUGHTS

For Breakfast Today I Had:

Today's Exercise/Physical Activity Was (State What It Was And For How Long):

For Lunch Today I Had:

Today's Compliment To Myself:

For Dinner Today I Had:

Today I Imagined Myself:

Today I Snacked On:

Although I Wanted To

_____, I

Today's Water Intake:

_____

_____.

Today's Supplements Were:

A Characteristic That I Am Choosing To Improve On:

Affirmation #111: I Always Give Off Good Energy.

DEDICATING THIS TIME IN MY LIFE TO TRANSFORMATION.

THE WEALTH IN MY HEALTH

MORNING ACTIONS AND THOUGHTS

Today:

Mood:

Today's Physical Goal:

Today I Need:

Today I Am Showing Appreciation To My Body By:

I Will Give Myself What I Need Today By:

Today I Am Choosing To Believe:

I Know I Do Not Need:

Today I Am Replacing An Old Belief With This New Belief (State The New Belief):

Today's Physical Activity Is:

I Will Support My New Beliefs By:

Today I Am Opening Up My Heart And Mind To:

Today's Blood Pressure: _____ Today's Sugar Count: _____

330

Continue To The Next Page

THE WEALTH IN MY HEALTH

For Breakfast Today I Had:

Today's Exercise/Physical Activity Was (State What It Was And For How Long):

For Lunch Today I Had:

Today's Compliment To Myself:

For Dinner Today I Had:

Today I Imagined Myself:

Today I Snacked On:

Although I Wanted To

_____, I

Today's Water Intake:

_____

_____.

Today's Supplements Were:

A Characteristic That I Am Choosing To Improve On:

THE WEALTH IN MY HEALTH

Today:

Mood:

Today's Physical Goal:

Today I Need:

Today I Am Showing Appreciation To My Body By:

I Will Give Myself What I Need Today By:

Today I Am Choosing To Believe:

I Know I Do Not Need:

Today I Am Replacing An Old Belief With This New Belief (State The New Belief):

Today's Physical Activity Is:

I Will Support My New Beliefs By:

Today I Am Opening Up My Heart And Mind To:

Today's Blood Pressure: _____ Today's Sugar Count: _____

332

Continue To The Next Page

THE WEALTH IN MY HEALTH

NIGHT ACTIONS AND THOUGHTS

For Breakfast Today I Had:

For Lunch Today I Had:

For Dinner Today I Had:

Today I Snacked On:

Today's Water Intake:

Today's Supplements Were:

Today's Exercise/Physical Activity Was (State What It Was And For How Long):

Today's Compliment To Myself:

Today I Imagined Myself:

Although I Wanted To

_____, I

_____

_____.

A Characteristic That I Am Choosing To Improve On:

THE WEALTH IN MY HEALTH
MORNING ACTIONS AND THOUGHTS

Today: Mood:

Today's Physical Goal:

Today I Need:

Today I Am Showing Appreciation To My Body By:

I Will Give Myself What I Need Today By:

Today I Am Choosing To Believe:

I Know I Do Not Need:

Today I Am Replacing An Old Belief With This New Belief (State The New Belief):

Today's Physical Activity Is:

I Will Support My New Beliefs By:

Today I Am Opening Up My Heart And Mind To:

Today's Blood Pressure: _____ Today's Sugar Count: _____

334   Continue To The Next Page

THE WEALTH IN MY HEALTH

For Breakfast Today I Had:

Today's Exercise/Physical Activity Was (State What It Was And For How Long):

For Lunch Today I Had:

Today's Compliment To Myself:

For Dinner Today I Had:

Today I Imagined Myself:

Today I Snacked On:

Although I Wanted To

_____, I

Today's Water Intake:

_____

_____.

Today's Supplements Were:

A Characteristic That I Am Choosing To Improve On:

THE WEALTH IN MY HEALTH

Today:

Mood:

Today's Physical Goal:

Today I Need:

Today I Am Showing Appreciation To My Body By:

I Will Give Myself What I Need Today By:

Today I Am Choosing To Believe:

I Know I Do Not Need:

Today I Am Replacing An Old Belief With This New Belief (State The New Belief):

Today's Physical Activity Is:

I Will Support My New Beliefs By:

Today I Am Opening Up My Heart And Mind To:

Today's Blood Pressure: _____ Today's Sugar Count: _____

336

Continue To The Next Page

THE WEALTH IN MY HEALTH

For Breakfast Today I Had:

Today's Exercise/Physical Activity Was (State What It Was And For How Long):

For Lunch Today I Had:

Today's Compliment To Myself:

For Dinner Today I Had:

Today I Imagined Myself:

Today I Snacked On:

Although I Wanted To

_____, I

Today's Water Intake:

_____

_____.

Today's Supplements Were:

A Characteristic That I Am Choosing To Improve On:

WHOLENESS NOTES

THE WEALTH IN MY HEALTH

Today: Mood:

Today's Physical Goal: Today I Need:

Today I Am Showing Appreciation To My   I Will Give Myself What I Need Today By:
Body By:

Today I Am Choosing To Believe: I Know I Do Not Need:

Today I Am Replacing An Old Belief With   Today's Physical Activity Is:
This New Belief (State The New Belief):

I Will Support My New Beliefs By: Today I Am Opening Up My Heart And
                                           Mind To:

Today's Blood Pressure: _____ Today's Sugar Count: _____

Continue To The Next Page

339

THE WEALTH IN MY HEALTH

For Breakfast Today I Had:

Today's Exercise/Physical Activity Was (State What It Was And For How Long):

For Lunch Today I Had:

Today's Compliment To Myself:

For Dinner Today I Had:

Today I Imagined Myself:

Today I Snacked On:

Although I Wanted To

_____, I

Today's Water Intake:

_____

_____.

Today's Supplements Were:

A Characteristic That I Am Choosing To Improve On:

Affirmation #116: I Now Take Excellent Care Of Myself Inside And Out.

THE WEALTH IN MY HEALTH

Today: Mood:

Today's Physical Goal: Today I Need:

Today I Am Showing Appreciation To My   I Will Give Myself What I Need Today By:
Body By:

Today I Am Choosing To Believe: I Know I Do Not Need:

Today I Am Replacing An Old Belief With   Today's Physical Activity Is:
This New Belief (State The New Belief):

I Will Support My New Beliefs By: Today I Am Opening Up My Heart And
                                            Mind To:

Today's Blood Pressure: _____ Today's Sugar Count: _____

THE WEALTH IN MY HEALTH

For Breakfast Today I Had:

Today's Exercise/Physical Activity Was (State What It Was And For How Long):

For Lunch Today I Had:

Today's Compliment To Myself:

For Dinner Today I Had:

Today I Imagined Myself:

Today I Snacked On:

Although I Wanted To

_____, I

Today's Water Intake:

_____

_____.

Today's Supplements Were:

A Characteristic That I Am Choosing To Improve On:

Affirmation #117: My Body Is A Gift.

I'VE DECIDED TO INVEST IN MY HEALTH BY

THE WEALTH IN MY HEALTH

MORNING ACTIONS AND THOUGHTS

Today: Mood:

Today's Physical Goal: Today I Need:

Today I Am Showing Appreciation To My   I Will Give Myself What I Need Today By:
Body By:

Today I Am Choosing To Believe: I Know I Do Not Need:

Today I Am Replacing An Old Belief With   Today's Physical Activity Is:
This New Belief (State The New Belief):

I Will Support My New Beliefs By: Today I Am Opening Up My Heart And
                                                Mind To:

Today's Blood Pressure: _____ Today's Sugar Count: _____

344   Continue To The Next Page

THE WEALTH IN MY HEALTH

For Breakfast Today I Had:

Today's Exercise/Physical Activity Was (State What It Was And For How Long):

For Lunch Today I Had:

Today's Compliment To Myself:

For Dinner Today I Had:

Today I Imagined Myself:

Today I Snacked On:

Although I Wanted To

_____, I

Today's Water Intake:

_____

_____.

Today's Supplements Were:

A Characteristic That I Am Choosing To Improve On:

THE WEALTH IN MY HEALTH

Today: | Mood:

Today's Physical Goal: | Today I Need:

Today I Am Showing Appreciation To My Body By: | I Will Give Myself What I Need Today By:

Today I Am Choosing To Believe: | I Know I Do Not Need:

Today I Am Replacing An Old Belief With This New Belief (State The New Belief): | Today's Physical Activity Is:

I Will Support My New Beliefs By: | Today I Am Opening Up My Heart And Mind To:

Today's Blood Pressure: _____ Today's Sugar Count: _____

346

Continue To The Next Page

THE WEALTH IN MY HEALTH

For Breakfast Today I Had:

Today's Exercise/Physical Activity Was (State What It Was And For How Long):

For Lunch Today I Had:

Today's Compliment To Myself:

For Dinner Today I Had:

Today I Imagined Myself:

Today I Snacked On:

Although I Wanted To

_____, I

Today's Water Intake:

_____

_____.

Today's Supplements Were:

A Characteristic That I Am Choosing To Improve On:

THE WEALTH IN MY HEALTH

MORNING ACTIONS AND THOUGHTS

Today:

Mood:

Today's Physical Goal:

Today I Need:

Today I Am Showing Appreciation To My Body By:

I Will Give Myself What I Need Today By:

Today I Am Choosing To Believe:

I Know I Do Not Need:

Today I Am Replacing An Old Belief With This New Belief (State The New Belief):

Today's Physical Activity Is:

I Will Support My New Beliefs By:

Today I Am Opening Up My Heart And Mind To:

Today's Blood Pressure: _____ Today's Sugar Count: _____

Continue To The Next Page

THE WEALTH IN MY HEALTH

For Breakfast Today I Had:

Today's Exercise/Physical Activity Was (State What It Was And For How Long):

For Lunch Today I Had:

Today's Compliment To Myself:

For Dinner Today I Had:

Today I Imagined Myself:

Today I Snacked On:

Although I Wanted To

_____, I

Today's Water Intake:

_____

_____.

Today's Supplements Were:

A Characteristic That I Am Choosing To Improve On: